Primer for Parents
of Preschoolers

Primer for Parents of Preschoolers

Edith G. Neisser

Parents' Magazine Press
New York

International Standard Book Number 0–8193–0618–5
Library of Congress Catalog Card Number 72–2315
**Produced for Parents' Magazine Press
by Stravon Educational Press**
Primer for Parents of Preschoolers is being published
in a special edition as *Guiding Your Preschooler*.
Manufactured in the United States of America

Contents

What Shall We Expect During These Years? • Each
Child Is Unique • The Pressures of Rapid Social Change
• The "Self-fulfilling Prophecy" • Acquiring Skills •
Essential Tasks of Growing • They Learn to Move More
Smoothly • Will They Slow Up? • Understanding and
Thinking Expand • Communication Becomes More Flu-
ent • Developing Communication • Reasoning Is Con-
crete and Personal • The Intricacies of Kinship Can Be
Puzzling • Inferences Seem Like Magic • Magic Think-
ing • Ideas About Time • Relations with Others • The
Contrasts in First Grade • Impulsiveness Decreases •
More People Included in Their Affections • They Want
to Grow Up, But . . .

How Can We Help? • Sources of Conflict Are Universal
• Learning to Share • The Wells of Affection Are Deep •
Unfamiliar Routines Are Upsetting • Getting Ready for a
New Baby • Timing the Announcement • When Baby-
hood Looks Like the Good Life • Safety Valves for Strong
Feelings • Some Alternatives • Forestalling Trouble •
Cultivating Friendliness • The Value of Separation •
"Being Fair" Can Be a Booby Trap • Half a Loaf Is Often
Better Than None • Not Position, But How It Is Dealt
With, Counts • Prestige and Pressure for the Eldest •
The "Only-Child" Hangover • Being in the Middle •
Special Privileges • Does It Pay to Be Youngest? • Boons
of a Large Family • Plaints of "Youngests" • Children
Learn from Each Other • "Only" Need Not Equal
"Lonely" • "Only" Can Be "Different" • Substitute Sib-
lings

Developing Sociability • Playmates Contribute to Growth
• Tolerance Is an Individual Matter • Stages in Friend-

v

liness • New Ideas from Playmates • Teaching Sharing
• Learning Takes Time • Stumbling Blocks to Friend-
liness • The Need for Reassurance • Helping to Foster
Sociability • How Skills Can Help • Tattling Versus
Responsible Reporting • Bullies Need Help • Helping
Ease Hidden Fears • Finding Playmates • Nursery School
or Alternatives • Supervising Play • Do It My Way—
Nicely • Enjoyment of Playing Alone Is Valuable • Man-
ners in Today's World • Nursery Schools • Other Kinds
of Nursery School • Judging a School

Discipline for the Young • Variety in Discipline • When
to Discard Old Rules • Fostering Cooperation • "No"
Does Not Always Mean "No" • Stability Is Reassuring •
Removing Temptation • Knowing What Is Expected
Helps • Freedom Within a Safe Framework • Taking
the Consequences • Consistency and Flexibility • De-
structive Inconsistency • When Adults Need to Be Firm
• Parents and Security • A Time and Place for Rewards
• The Delayed Reward • Punishment: A Last Resort •
Chronic Disobedience • Trying to Communicate • Bal-
ancing Controls • Respecting the Child

Questions Serve Numerous Purposes • Conversation
Starters • When a Question Is Not THE Question •
Questions About Family Crises • The Stalling Device •
Information-seeking Questions • Clearing Up Confusion
• Questions About Conduct • When to Tell the Truth
About Myths • "Where Do Babies Come From?" •
Understand the Question • Using Correct Terms • Just
Give the Facts • Different but Equal • When a Child
Asks No Questions • Learning from Questioning

Expectations and Behavior • What Makes the Difference?
• Stereotypes Get in Our Way • Forcing Responsibility
• How Children See Their Parents • Are We Unfair to
Our Girls? • Do Boys Pay a Price for Privilege? • How
Does Sexual Identity Develop? • Parental Behavior and
the Identification Process • The Family Romance •

Preface

READING ABOUT HOW small children grow through love and friction with the people around them can be thought-provoking and fun. The presentation in this volume of the preschooler's nature, his needs, and his relationships has been arranged so that you may readily turn to a particular topic or problem that concerns your family at the moment, or get a panorama of the development of the years from three through five by reading the entire book.

Chapter 1 gives you an overview of the child's development in size and strength, in ability to reason and to learn, to get along with others, and to express and control feelings in serviceabe ways.

The next three chapters trace a youngster's relationships with his brothers and sisters (Chapter 2), his contemporaries (Chapter 3), and with adults who represent authority (Chapter 4). The latter chapter takes up the kind of discipline in the family that tends to keep the inevitable contrariness of these years within bounds.

The next two chapters are related. Chapter 5 is concerned with gratifying and keeping alive your child's curiosity in all directions, as well as answering his questions about the differences between boys and girls and where babies come from. The consideration of those questions leads into the following chapter, which involves the way young children develop pride in their own sex membership and learn to value both sexes.

Chapters 7 and 8 could well be read together, since fears are not always generated by real events. Frequently they are the result of disquieting inner feelings that originate in a newly acquired and too busy conscience.

Independence, the subject of Chapter 9, rests on a child's having sufficient freedom from fear so that he may move toward becoming a self-propelling boy or girl.

Development does not proceed smoothly for every child throughout these years, so minor annoyances and larger worries are taken up in Chapter 10. References to this chapter will be found in earlier ones. These and other cross-references are worth following up, for all a child's experiences and relationships are so interdependent that one cannot isolate a topic.

Preparing your child for school is the subject of the final chapter.

If you look up a subject in the Index, you will probably find several references. Again, no bit of behavior is made out of whole cloth but is part of the patchwork design that is the total personality. You will probably discover, for that reason, that the pages the Index leads you to, when read by themselves, are usually less illuminating than a complete chapter or two.

You will probably choose to read and reread sections of the volume from time to time, but we hope you will also read the book as a whole. As you see the different phases of growth in relation to each other, your own understanding of and pleasure in your preschoolers can be increased.

1

The
Delightful
Age

BETWEEN THEIR THIRD and sixth birthdays children are usually delightful, at least much of the time. Their refreshing naiveté and surprising perceptiveness make them good company. Their outspoken affection and admiration for their parents make them responsive and endearing. Mature enough to be fairly reliable in a number of domestic situations, they are still sufficiently home-centered not to give their parents the causes for concern that they may create a few years later when their whereabouts are harder to keep track of and their performance in school or in the neighborhood may leave something to be desired.

Their swift development on all fronts during these years also makes life with the three- through five-year-old exciting and fascinating—if at times exhausting. The six-year-old, twice as old as he was at three, is in

11

many respects twice as knowledgeable and competent. Not until the big spurt of growth at puberty that ushers in adolescence will so much dramatic change again occur in so brief a period as in these years, which, for want of a better term, we call "preschool."

In some ways, this period foreshadows adolescence and is, in a sense, a rehearsal for it. The young child unwittingly is practicing, on a small scale and in the relatively safe setting of home, the independence and self-assertion, the establishment of himself or herself as a member of his or her own sex that characterize and complicate the teens. The efforts we put into helping the preschooler master the tasks in development, acquire the skills, and form the relationships suitable to this period pay off a decade later as well as in the present. A good life from three through five is a sound foundation for weathering the proverbial storms of adolescence.

What Shall We Expect During These Years?

How, in general, may preschoolers be expected to develop in body, in mind, in feelings, and in ability to get along with others?

Right here, we need to recognize two points. Physical, mental, social, and emotional attributes are so intertwined, and their growth is so integrated, that in separating them for purposes of discussion we may lose an important dimension. One cannot say, "This boy, or this girl, cannot play happily with other children," as if that amply described the whole problem. The child may be suffering from hunger or fatigue, or intense fear, or all-consuming anger, or lack of confidence in himself or in the world around him. Similarly, we cannot assume that a child is failing to grasp an idea or master a skill solely because his mental powers are not equal to doing so. In order to learn, a young child needs to feel at ease with himself and with others and be free from persistent physical discomfort.

The second point to keep in mind is the importance of individual differences. We may suggest a *range* of behavior and attitudes likely to occur during these years and some responses typical of youngsters in this phase of development. Yet, children, even in the same family, differ so greatly that no two will exhibit the same traits or react in the same manner to similar situations.

Each Child Is Unique

These sharp individual differences stem from the infinite combination of physical characteristics and tendencies that may be inherited and from the difference in experience and environment that is each child's lot. The uniqueness of each family unit is obvious, but we tend to lose sight of how dissimilar the surroundings are even for children growing up under the same roof with the same parents. Each has his own position in birth order (which is discussed further in Chapter 2), with all that that entails.

Each benefits from a different degree of experience in his parents and a different measure of enthusiasm for bringing up children. Everything that is happening to those parents forms a part of the child's environment. Their health, their satisfaction or lack of it in their work, their friends, and their relatives will color the background against which a boy or girl develops. Parents' involvement or distress over larger issues in the neighborhood or the nation also has an impact.

The Pressures of Rapid Social Change

One condition affecting everyone in our society today is the overpowering swiftness of change, as Alvin Toffler documents in *Future Shock*. Adults, continually bombarded with unassimilable alterations in many phases of their lives, are less able to cope than they might be in a more stable world. Their inner equilibrium is thrown off balance. Small children feel the impact of the resulting anxious uncertainty in their parents.

Add this acceleration in the outer world to the child's own changes within his vastly expanding mental, social, and emotional boundaries, and one can understand the degree of pressure under which most preschoolers today are growing up.

The "Self-fulfilling Prophecy"

Other influences also contribute to the unique flavor of each personality. One of these has been labeled by Ralph Linton, an anthropologist, the "self-fulfilling prophecy." Parents form different expectations for each of their children. Whether or not they mean to, they push their young toward the fulfillment of those expectations.

"She's been shy since the day she was born," says a father of his four-year-old daughter. Now that the girl and her parents are convinced of her timidity, it is impossible to tell whether she has assumed the shrinking-violet role because it was imposed on her, or whether some inborn sensitivity has impelled her to shrink from new situations and strangers to a degree unusual for her age.

Because of the great individual variation among youngsters, especially during these years, and because so much growing takes place in so many directions, any overview must necessarily convey only a rough and sketchy idea of the changes in behavior and attainments that may occur.

Acquiring Skills

We cannot force growth, as that comes from within the individual, but we can provide a setting congenial to it.

We can take advantage of those periods in a youngster's life when he acquires certain skills quite easily and is ready for the new step. Usually, he gives some signal. He may put his readiness into words: "Can do self." Sometimes, he may simply go ahead and try the new step on his own.

Another indication that a specific kind of learning should not be delayed too long: there is evidence that some children who cannot stay dry during the night at four or five years of age had their toilet training delayed beyond the age of two-and-a-half or even three. Possibly delayed toilet training is partly responsible for bedwetting. (Chapter 9 goes into this question in greater detail.)

Essential Tasks of Growing

Not only are there favorable times for acquiring certain skills, but children also need to accomplish specific social and emotional tasks during stated periods.

Mastery of these tasks lays a firm foundation for subsequent development. Otherwise, there may be weak spots in the personality that can be troublesome later.

One of the basic tasks for preschoolers, according to Erik Erikson, is the development of initiative, the discovery that they can safely try out their powers. The exploring, experimenting, and questioning to which the three-, four-, and five-year-olds devote themselves are ways in which they exercise initiative. In providing suitable opportunities for such activity, we are also supplying the setting for healthy growth. (More about this in Chapters 5 and 6.)

Along with initative goes some guilt at times. The youngster is delighted with his recently acquired ability to run and climb, open and shut doors and drawers, lift and carry objects, put together and take apart whatever comes to hand, mold and shape malleable substances. All these activities are really forms of attack, conquest, and possession. In his imagination he becomes Batman or a ferocious beast and plays at, or daydreams about, all manner of daring exploits. Deep inside himself, he knows he cannot, and must not, carry out his imaginings. He often becomes frightened and guilty because he has thought about being so powerful. A mild degree of guilt helps him become more "civilized." (See Chapter 7.)

Because preschoolers are ready to exercise some initiative, they are ready for greater independence. They also profit from experiences in which they can employ their new-found competencies. Some of our conflicts with them stem from our underestimating how much they can do for and by themselves. (For examples, see

Chapters 4 and 9.)

One more growing job is to discover which sex one belongs to and that being either a boy or a girl is good. (This is the subject of Chapter 6.)

They Learn to Move More Smoothly

Development goes from the simple to the more complex and tends toward specialization in the use of muscles during these years. For instance, as he turns three, a youngster is still satisfied with banging a spoon on a pan or putting small saucepans inside larger ones and carrying them around not too steadily. He clutches objects he handles. As the coordination of the small muscles in his hands improves—and he becomes able to sit still for a few minutes—he enjoys fitting simple puzzles together. He uses a hammer, at first just to pound, but soon to make an "airplane" out of two pieces of wood nailed together. He tries drawing with a crayon or pencil, can hold one quite readily and draw a crude figure with it.

Before he is six, he may try copying letters or printing his name. The two sticks nailed together no longer satisfy his desire to make an airplane. Now he can use a small saw or a coping saw. He tries to make more complicated airplanes or boats.

Paintings go from being mere blobs of color to being attempts to portray houses and trees or "scenes" that tell, roughly, a story. Block building, for both boys and girls, goes from a few blocks piled precariously one on the other to the intricate structures that five-year-olds like to leave standing for several days.

Greater specialization in the use of the large

muscles of the trunk, legs, and arms also appears. Toddlers really "toddle," but the three-year-old strides along nimbly. By the time he is four or four-and-a-half he no longer puts his hands on the door frame to pull himself around a corner at top speed. Outdoors, the three-and-a-half-year-old becomes adept at climbing to the top of the jungle gym, if he has access to one. Before long, he tries swinging from one of the cross bars. On the swings, he can learn to propel himself by "pumping." For evidence of the physical development during these years, compare the performance of the five-and-a-half-year-old on the trapeze, the slide, the rings, and the climbing apparatus, where he is thoroughly at home and full of new tricks, with his hesitant approach to the playground about two years earlier.

Will They Slow Up?

If his parents are good walkers or climbers, the five-year-old has the stamina he lacked earlier to accompany them on short rambles. At four, he might have wilted on such excursions, and at three perhaps needed to be carried on the way home. Surefooted as he seems to be as he scrambles over rocks or climbs fences adroitly, the five-year-old still needs watching to keep him safe.

The increased coordination of the four-year-old is demonstrated by his ability to spin like a top, to hop, and, by the time he turns five, to skip. To go up and down stairs without putting both feet on a tread at the same time, and—dubious though the achievement may be in the eyes of the parents—to slide down the bannisters are among the typically "fourish" achievements.

Many a four- and five-year-old has both the flexibility and the coordination it takes to sit cross-legged with the foot of one leg on top of the knee of the other. Mothers, if they have been intrigued by yoga exercises, may try in vain to imitate this "lotus position."

Both girls and boys, during these years, like to imitate dance steps they have seen on television. They do so with increasing ease and grace. The fives seem so well able to keep in step that fond relatives are prompted to suggest that dancing lessons are now in order.

The five-year-old, if family finances permit or a hand-me-down is available, can usually graduate from a tricycle to a two-wheeler. Swimming, diving, and roller- or ice-skating in clumsy fashion may be attempted at four and almost mastered at five. Three-year-old swimmers, among those who have the chance to swim all year long, are not rare. L. Joseph Stone and Joseph Church, in *Childhood and Adolescence*, describe the alterations in appearance that accompany the preschooler's physical development:

His proportions are changing. His legs grow faster than the rest of him. At age two they account for 34% of his length; by age 5, 44%, which approaches the half-and-half proportions of the adult. . . . As his legs lengthen and head growth slows drastically, he loses the top-heavy look of infancy and toddlerhood. As the cartilage and bones of his face develop, and the fat pads in his cheeks dwindle, his countenance loses its babyish cast and becomes better defined and more like his adult self.

Understanding and Thinking Expand

Physical and mental growth combine, in the almost-six-year-old, to give him the capacity to grasp the fact that some feats are impossible because of his lack of skill, not because they are forbidden. Youngsters, before they leave the preschool period behind, have gained a degree of self-knowledge. They have learned something of their own limitations. They may have gone through, around four, a spell of braggadocio in which they assert their prowess in exaggerated statements. At five and a half, they may say quite realistically, "I can't do that," or, as one beautifully self-confident little girl put it, "I haven't learned to do that yet."

The five-year-old's sense of being himself, an individual who belongs to a particular family, has blossomed beyond what it was two years earlier. Ask a five-year-old where he lives and he will probably not only give you the street address but proudly add the city and state as well. That their country is composed of fifty states is too involved for most five-year-olds to understand, although they struggle with the concept of towns within states and states within the nation.

Communication Becomes More Fluent

As a conversationalist, the youngster at the end of the preschool years has gone far. At three, he may still have had a baby lisp, been unable to pronounce certain sounds, and had a limited and factual vocabulary. He could name many *things* around him, but the intangible eluded him.

At four he probably took pleasure in making up silly words that sent him and his contemporaries into uproarious laughter. "It's ugly. It's an ugly-pugly," says a four-year-old holding a worm in his hand.

"It's an ugly-pugly-wuggly wormy-squirmy-germy," says his companion, and both are off on a spree of nonsense rhyming.

The "how?" "when?" "why?" "what for?" and "who?" questions reach a peak when a youngster is around four and frequently are a source of exasperation to parents. Asking, and feeling that it is acceptable to ask, facilitates mental growth. (Chapter 5 is concerned with this subject.)

Developing Communication

In both clarity of pronunciation and fluency the advance from three- or four- to five-year-old ability is highlighted by what transpires in "Show and Tell" in kindergarten and nursery school. Kindergartners are eager to bring to school interesting subjects and to communicate facts.

"We haven't named our kittens yet, an' my Dad says we can't keep them all an' their mother borned them yesterday an' when we couldn't find her she was in Mr. Foster's Chevy an' he lives next door to us an' he was mad!" may not be a model of lucid narrative, but it is a more intelligible kindergarten type of account than was given by that narrator's younger sister to her nursery schoolmates. Her version was, "Pansy's babies were in Mr. Foster's back seat and she licked them clean and he told my daddy a lot of bad words about Pansy. You know what he said? He said to my Daddy . . ." At this point the nursery school teacher, with a fairly good idea of what the irate Mr. Foster said, broke in to ask how many kittens there were. "Oh, lots and lots, like zillions," was the answer, since to a four-year-old, five is as much as a zillion.

The kindergartner, when asked the same question, answered, "I have to think. Maybe I don't know. They were sort of brown and white, I guess."

Even a bright four-year-old has difficulty in dealing with the fact that an object or a group of objects has color, size, and weight, and that in the case of a group, number, too, is one of its attributes. That the biggest may not be the heaviest, or the oldest, if animals or people are involved, is also confusing. Around the time boys and girls enter first grade, they usually have some notion that a group of objects or people may be alike in one respect but different in others, but they are not yet at home with this concept.

Show a five-and-a-half-year-old a jumble of triangular and square blocks of various sizes and colors and ask him to group together those that are of the same shape, or size, or color, and he may be able to do it. Intricate classification is often beyond him. A year later he will probably have mastered the concept of classification.

Reasoning Is Concrete and Personal

The title of the delightful children's book *A Hole Is To Dig*, by Ruth Krauss, is an example of how a three- or four-year-old perceives objects. Asked "What is a hole?" or "What is a cat?" he will probably tell you one thing about it, the thing that is most important to him at the moment. "A hole is to dig," if he likes to dig; "A cat is to pet," or "A cat is to have kittens," if kittens fascinate him (not because he has any feeling for the ongoing quality of life). His thinking is egocentric and centered on the particular and concrete.

The five-year-old might tell you that a cat likes milk, or that cats scratch, or that his cat is named Nipper, but he would not be able to answer that question by saying, "A cat is an animal," nor would the fact that a cat lives in a house with people be significant to him.

The Intricacies of Kinship Can Be Puzzling

Classification of objects and animals is not as perplexing as the relationships of members of the family, which throw the three- and four-year-old completely. The increase in four-generation families has made complications for some children. The fact that great-grandmother is the mother of grandma is incredible, for both women look pretty much the same age to their youngest descendants. Besides, how could grandma ever have been a child with a mother of her own? That a child's father is also the uncle of several children varying greatly in age and size is also hard to understand. The custom of some husbands and wives of calling each other "mother" and "father" does not help the preschool child get relationships straight, either. Youngsters who must cope with the concept of stepparents, stepbrothers, and stepsisters get relationships really tangled.

By the time a child is "going on six," if he has had patient explanations of family relationships and is well acquainted with relatives bearing different labels, kinship patterns tend to become clearer.

Inferences Seem Like Magic

The inferences through which adults arrive at conclusions, see "cause and effect" relationships, seem magical to preschoolers.

"I want to go to Roddy's house," says a four-and-a-half-year-old, as he and his mother start out for the supermarket.

"Roddy won't be home now," says his mother.

"How do *you* know?" says the small skeptic.

Since they will pass Roddy's house anyway, Mother consents to ring the bell, and, as she predicted, nobody is home.

The four-and-a-half-year-old is impressed. "You are a magic-mommy," he says in astonishment.

"No magic. I know Roddy and his mother almost always go to his grandmother's on Wednesday, and this is Wednesday. See?"

Magic Thinking

The preschooler's primitive "magic thinking" also shows in his tendency to endow toys and other objects with feelings. A four-year-old will say, "My dolly was lonesome, so I'm telling her a story," or "That spoon is bad. It keeps falling down on the floor. Spoon, I'm going to spank you if you fall down again."

Imaginary companions who play a large part in the lives of many three-and-a-half- and four-year-olds usually begin to fade out (often with a violent end, like being lost in a sewer) from the thinking of five-and-a-half-year-olds.

Another facet of magic thinking is the tendency of three-, four-, and to some extent five-year-olds to attribute everything that occurs to somebody's arranging it. "Why did they make it snow today?" or "Why do they make leaves fall off trees?" That is about as far as they get with cause and effect in the preschool years, but they are on their way.

As set forth in detail in Chapter 7, preschoolers have an unreal conception of their own responsibility for "bad things" that may happen. They equate thinking about something bad with doing something bad. The fives are still troubled by the fear that they have brought about catastrophe, if it strikes them even indirectly. Whether any of us gets over this notion completely is an interesting question.

Ideas About Time

Preschool children are "here-and-now" creatures. Three-year-olds distinguish morning, afternoon, and night, but "day after tomorrow" or "next week" are impossible for them to envisage. "At supper time" or "After one more sleep" have more meaning than "six o'clock" or "tomorrow." Five-year-olds can join in the planning for the next day, or a few days ahead, but "next summer" is too distant to be real. They may know the hour they go to bed or the time they get up in the morning, but a more detailed awareness of time is usually not within their scope, though this depends somewhat on how "time-conscious" the household is. For a preschooler to wait an hour for his father to come home is as trying as for his father to wait all day for a cup of coffee.

To look back to a time when he was not alive is difficult, even at five. The boy who asked his grandfather, "What did you watch before there was TV?" could not comprehend a world so different from his own that it offered nothing "to watch." If the kindergartner attempts to consider history, he tends to telescope Washington, Lincoln, and "before there were moon landings" into a mysterious dark age.

Five-year-olds have come far, but they may deceive us by glibly using terms they have picked up from older children or TV and which they do not really understand. Because they pay attention to inconsequential details to which preoccupied adults are oblivious, they may appear to have astonishing memories. Our son or daughter may be able to tell us the color of the automobile of a visitor a week ago or recall that "Mommy had on her pink scarf last time she took me to the dentist." If we try to skip part of a well-loved story, the older preschoolers will probably catch us and insist on the authentic version!

Relations with Others

To gain an idea of how far youngsters have come in their ability to get along with others between age three and the end of age five, contrast the first day of a group of threes in nursery school with opening day in first grade.

The nursery school probably requires that a parent or someone the child knows well remain with him during the first session. Many of the children stay quite close to the adult who brought them. They pay scant attention to the other children, and not much more to the teacher. When one child does approach another, he may touch, pinch, or prod, rather than talk. Communication is likely to be in brief phrases. Exploration of the play materials and the nursery school setup, except on the part of the most self-assured, is likely to be tentative, in spite of encouragement from the teacher and her assistants.

Two or three children may play alongside each other, but cooperative play, in which views are exchanged and each child takes a definite role, is not to be expected in the first weeks of nursery school. (More about this in Chapter 3.)

Snatching toys away from another child or preempting a firetruck or a doll bed and refusing to relinquish it is the play style for the majority of children on the first day. Tears or a show of anger are near the surface for many of the youngsters from time to time and frequently break out.

The Contrasts in First Grade

Now look at the first-grader who is probably left at the door of the classroom by a parent or an older brother or sister. He is likely to be proud of coming to first grade, even if somewhat awed by it.

He understands that his teacher will be the authority and that his parents are not the only adults to whom he listens. He may listen to his teacher eagerly, fearfully, or sullenly, but he listens.

The rather aimless exploration of surroundings that characterized the three-year-old on his first day in nursery school has been replaced, for most first-graders, by a purposeful examination of the classroom. The boys and girls understand the use of the materials they find, such as books, paper, crayons, chalk boards, and chalk. If there are fish in an aquarium or other kinds of pets or plants, pictures on bulletin boards, or shells, rocks,

pumpkins, or autumn leaves on display, the child may comment, often critically, on them.

If the teacher hands out drawing materials and allows a free choice of subjects, most of the children will have an idea of what they want to draw before they begin. The scrawling and scribbling of the three-year-olds has been left behind.

Many first-graders may be shy the first day, but chattiness and an effort to impress others are also present. If members of the class have been together in kindergarten or know one another from neighborhood play, "best friends" may gravitate toward one another. Conversations, establishing where one lives, one's name.

and, to some degree, one's competence and sophistication as to TV programs, are struck up between new aquaintances. Cooperative play comes easily to most, although arguments and cries of "No fair," "You cheater, you!" and similar complaints abound.

Impulsiveness Decreases

Discussing the changes in his daughter and her friends between their third and sixth birthdays, a father said:

At three they belonged to the "I want what I want when I want it" school of thought. They couldn't wait. They were entirely creatures of impulse. I wouldn't say they are exactly patient now, but they aren't quite as quick to fly into a rage or panic if they have to wait. They may ask twenty times, "When will my Mommy be here?" but they are not so likely to weep or say Mommy is bad or they don't love her any more.

A mother who was asked what changes she felt were significant in her youngsters' response to their contemporaries during these years, named the development of sympathy as one of the salient advances:

By the age of five, you could see what was really sympathy showing up. One youngster would comfort another who had been mistreated, or would come and look for me so I could do something. Of course, that didn't mean that the one who showed sympathy today wouldn't dish out a bit of mistreatment tomorrow.

As Stone and Church point out, sympathy is allied to leadership, another social trait that emerges in many youngsters, in different forms, around the age of five. Both traits come out of a rudimentary understanding of how other children feel and a capacity for responding to their feelings.

Although violent outbursts and tantrums tend to diminish and often disappear in emotionally healthy children during the later preschool years, boys and girls have by no means attained stability or serenity. Their feelings are still changeable, frequently overwhelming. A five-year-old may have more fears than he had at three, as both his understanding of real events and his ability to conjure up imaginary dangers have increased. (Chapters 7 and 8 deal with this.)

More People Included in Their Affections

The five-year-old's capacity for giving affection has expanded. Adults among his relatives and outside the family are included in his affections and fondly talked of when they are absent from his circle. A favorite aunt may be wanted at a birthday party. A friendly neighbor may find our five-year-old on her doorstep at all hours of the day.

The fours and fives have advanced beyond regarding their contemporaries as little more than objects, but they enjoy one another's company for what each can add to an undertaking. There is a strong flavor of opportunism and hardly a trace of loyalty in the "friendships" of five-year-olds. "I miss Tammy awfully," says her neighbor, aged four and a half, but when Tammy returns from her brief stay with a grandparent and goes next door to find this friend who could not wait for her return, the friend may be playing with another child and not inclined to include Tammy in what is going on. Social skills, except in a few children who seem to be positively gifted that way, are not in the repertoire of the four- and five-year-olds.

They Want to Grow Up, But . . .

Fresh attainments bring a preschooler pride and satisfaction. Sometimes the five-year-old seems to be operating on a level so much beyond his usual performance that we may say of him, "He is doing better than he knows how to do."

Yet sometimes, with visible relief, he will slide back to a more babyish form of response or activity. This retreat may be in the service of development. Perhaps he needs a rest, socially and emotionally, so that he can pull himself together and once more forge ahead. Development is not an ever-upward process.

Our children are probably growing more than we are aware of in our day-to-day dealings with them. We can afford, much of the time, to trust the forces of growth and development if we provide a good setting for them.

An old song goes, "Turn around and you're two,/ Turn around and you're four,/Turn around and you're a young man going out of my door." And indeed, our five-year-old, as he turns six, is, in his own fashion and at his own level, as he enters first grade, a young man going out of our door.

2

When There Are Siblings—and When There Are None

THE CURRENTS OF feeling that flow back and forth between brothers and sisters etch a pattern into the life of the family and into the personality of each of the children. At times, these feelings are predominantly charged with affection and admiration, at other times with anger and envy. They may influence a youngster's attitudes toward other people as he is growing up— even throughout his life.

Both love and resentment toward a brother or sister are likely to exist at the same moment. Contradictory feelings may be so mingled that behavior is inconsistent. The dilemma of one four-year-old may have a familiar ring. This little girl complained to her mother that an older sister was "a mean old boss."

"Then don't play with her this afternoon. You

can play by yourself or with your friend Ruthie," said the mother.

"Oh, no, I won't do *that!* I have more fun with Sis," was the answer.

Here is one condition that cannot be blamed on present-day developments! As legend and folklore attest, conflict between children in the family has existed since the beginning of time and in all known societies in which one mother takes care of several children.

From what sources do these currents of feeling flow? What are some approaches that may prove useful when a new baby is expected?

How Can We Help?

How can parents help a young child handle his feelings of rivalry so that he is not overwhelmed by them?

What steps can parents take to cultivate friendliness between the children?

To what extent does the position of being eldest, in the middle, or youngest color a child's picture of himself and influence his behavior?

What attitudes and what practical measures will tend to help each child enjoy the benefits and reduce the hazards inherent in his position?

Since the first child in a family is for a time an only child, how can the potential handicaps of being an "only," temporarily or permanently, be overcome?

Final answers to these questions are hardly possible, yet increased understanding of the complex relationship of those who share the same parents may help ease feelings all around.

Sources of Conflict Are Universal

Rivalry can be toned down but not prevented entirely, even though we "do all the right things." Indeed, a certain amount of resentment between the children in the family can be the means of their learning how to control and express competitiveness and aggressive feelings in constructive, socially useful ways.

A small child is possessive. He would like nothing better than to have mother and father all to himself. Sharing anything is hard, but sharing one's parents is all but unbearable in the early years. Look at the way the most amiable three-year-old strives for attention when his mother and a neighbor are having a cup of coffee and he is excluded from the conversation. The small child does not comprehend that parental affection expands to meet the demands of several children. Neither do the three to fives like to give. They much prefer being on the receiving end of good things, tangible and intangible. Yet, in countless ways they are required to give to both younger and elder brothers and sisters in the course of any day—a second source of friction.

Learning to Share

Sharing and giving need to be learned through experiences that are not intolerable. Such learning takes place with less pain and greater psychic economy within a friendly, accepting family.

Competition is characteristic of our society. Some students of human behavior say that this reflects the universal early struggles among the young to capture parental affection. Others say that competitiveness is fostered because adults introduce the techniques of the market place into family life, turning it into a rat race. Certainly, "Let's see who can do the best," or "Are you going to let your sister get ahead of you?" as a theme in family life heightens competition. Probably competitiveness stems from both inner and outer pressures, but in either case it is a further source of resentment between children in a family.

A more obvious reason for antagonisms was pointed out by a father after a long weekend at home with a three-year-old and a four-and-a-half-year-old. "No wonder our boys are always grabbing things away from each other and tattling," he said to his wife. "Do you realize how much they are together? Just being with *anybody* that steadily would make you snap at him pretty often. When one of them says to the other 'Go away!' maybe he's suffering from an overdose of brother."

The Wells of Affection Are Deep

Both the human condition and the way our lives are organized make a certain amount of resentment between the children inevitable, but at the same time, powerful bonds of affection also exist. Over and over, one child identifies with the sorrows or disappointments, the achievements or good fortune of another and grows closer to that one in doing so.

When five-year-old Patsy, whose older sister had had a bad fall, said to their mother, "Em needs you tonight. She'd feel better if you slept in my bed and I'll sleep in the living room on the couch," she demonstrated sincere concern for Em's welfare.

Solidarity often is enhanced by the alliances the children form and the conspiracies they hatch against their elders. Because they discover they can rely on one another at times, a mutuality takes root, although it may be a long time blossoming.

No matter how much the children may quarrel among themselves, let a child who is an outsider attack one of them, and the others in the family will rush to aid the victim—at least most of the time. Even an accusation of wrongdoing or a reprimand from an adult directed at one youngster may rally the others to his defense. Of course, that does not happen invariably. One brother or sister may gloat over another's being out of favor today and then take his part against the grown-ups tomorrow. Each time two or more become allies, their loyalty to one another tends to be reinforced.

Unfamiliar Routines Are Upsetting

A third strong force drawing the children together at an early age, although it is not always apparent, is their conviction that the rules and customs of their own home are the "right" and only way for life to be conducted. When a brother and sister went to stay with neighbors for a few days while their parents were away, they were distressed because routines were different from those to which they were accustomed. Still, their shared knowledge that baths should be taken before supper, and not at bedtime as their hostess decreed, or that eggs and bacon were the proper fare for breakfast and not for lunch, sustained them and raised the confidence each had in the other.

An indirect bit of evidence that children are more

attached to those with whom they are growing up than one might suppose is cited in *Review of Child Development Research* by Martin L. and Lois W. Hoffman. Children's choice of playmates tends to mirror the setup in their own families. Eldest children are more likely than others to play with younger ones. Considering that at an early age the eldest is often already quick to complain about having to play with or watch out for his juniors, such choice is, indeed, surprising. "Also," say the Hoffmans, "though children generally prefer others of the same sex as playmates, preference for those of the opposite sex was more frequently expressed by those with a sibling of the opposite sex than by those without."

Out of incidents in which children identify themselves with the feelings of one another and provide mutual emotional support and care, brotherly—and sisterly—love grows. It is an emotion parents need to tend, while accepting the inevitability of rivalry. The mere fact that some anger and jealousy are unpreventable does not mean that unlimited quantities of destructive behavior need be tolerated. Since opportunities to build friendliness are frequent, let us examine how we can turn them to good account.

Getting Ready for a New Baby

When the announcement is made to a small child that a brother or sister will be added to the family, how does he view it? If he is the only offspring, he may interpret his parents' reason for "wanting another" as evidence that he himself is less than satisfactory. To a three- or four-year-old, not liking what one has is the obvious reason for wanting another, be it a toy, a pair of shoes, or a friend.

Realizing how dubious the value of this anticipated addition seems to a small child, parents are sometimes tempted to resort to overselling the immediate benefits. The new baby will not be a playmate for a long time, nor will he, for the most part, be "lots of fun to have around" for his elder brother or sister. Parents can save themselves and their eldest some bad moments if they do not put themselves in a position in which their child can say, "You fooled me." One father relates:

> We learned the hard way that tricks backfire. Asking "Wouldn't you like to have a baby sister?" or saying, "It will be your baby," are really pretty shabby tricks. Much better to let the older one get angry at Mommy and Daddy for having such a foolish idea as having another baby than to pretend the decision was his.

Timing the Announcement

The months of pregnancy are long for everyone, especially for the young child to whom a few weeks can seem an eternity. Too early an announcement is unnecessary, but just when he shall be told the news depends, among other things, on how many changes in his life will be taking place because of the new arrival. He needs at least a few weeks or a month or two to become accustomed to the idea. One mother reports:

> The smartest thing I ever did was to let Pete see two or three small babies being fed and bathed and

cared for. Seeing those other babies cuddled by their mothers was no threat to Pete, and the first-hand acquaintance with how utterly helpless they were dispelled any illusions about what a newborn baby is like. I told him that he had been a baby and I had taken care of him just that way, so he knew he hadn't lost out on anything.

A nice balance can be maintained between making preparations for the coming event a part of family life and letting those preparations become the central fact in existence. A small child enjoys assisting in washing and sorting baby clothes when they are brought out of storage, helping to rearrange furniture to accommodate the refurbished crib, and similar homely matters. (Answering questions of the "Where is the baby now?" variety is discussed in Chapter 4.)

A youngster usually fares better if the timing of major adjustments such as starting nursery school, or giving up his bed with sides for a full-sized bed, occur well before the baby is on the scene. If he has a chance to become acquainted with the person who will take care of him while his mother is in the hospital, that separation will be less difficult.

A good-bye from mother when she departs for delivery will tend to prevent the feeling that she has just vanished.

When Babyhood Looks Like the Good Life

In spite of all precautions, a baby in the house calls for sharp changes in daily life. The nature, the timing, and the intensity of the protest against these changes on the part of those archconservatives, the preschool youngsters, vary from family to family. For each child, dissatisfaction comes and goes. Each will, at times, take delight in "helping" with the baby's care, admiring minute toes and fingers, exclaiming over a first smile, but each will also at times decide that "being big" is flat, stale, and unprofitable, as three-year-old Sheila did. To her, it seemed that the baby was loved and played with precisely because he was helpless. If demanding a bottle, crying frequently, and wetting and soiling were the way to her parents' heart, she too would be helpless.

Sheila's parents were inclined to hold the little girl sternly to standards they knew she could meet. When this only added to her misery and uncooperativeness, they listened to an older relative who had lived through similar behavior while rearing her own children: "Give Sheila all the comfort you can, is my advice. Tell her, 'O.K. We'll let you be like a baby in some ways for a while, but being three years old is really more fun.' Go along some of the way—like letting her have a bottle occasionally, zipping zippers for her, and that sort of thing, but don't let her beat a complete retreat. And you'd better prove to her that being her age is worth the effort. You know, let her go places with her father on Saturdays or Sundays. And eat dinner with you sometimes instead of having to go to sleep at six o'clock the way a baby does."

Safety Valves for Strong Feelings

Some children will suggest that having had the baby in the house for a few weeks is enough of such nonsense and it's time he was sent back to the hospital or disposed of in some less humanitarian fashion. Some few youngsters attempt such a disposal on their own. Others may deny the baby exists or ignore him entirely. Some may be extravagantly solicitous, literally trying to smother him with love.

A new baby brings a few problems in his wake for parents, too, and being urged to devote more time to playing with, reading to, or just cuddling the other young ones may seem more than can be expected of anyone. Still, the best investment mothers and fathers can make of their time often is to help those members of the family recently out of babyhood feel wanted, approved of, and "special."

A young child is sustained, too, by knowing that the parents accept his anger, and that his resentment against the baby is quite usual. "It's all right if you don't like your new brother sometimes. When I was as big as you are, I got mad at babies too, but after a while I got to like my sister and brother. You can tell me how you feel, but I won't let you do anything to hurt the baby." Statements along such lines offer a small child the protection he needs when his jealousy becomes frighteningly intense. Happily, children frequently find safety valves of their own.

Some Alternatives

Small girls may turn to dolls, and both boys and girls may use stuffed animals or puppets as objects of tender care or as babies who are soundly spanked because "This one is so bad today I can't stand it any more."

Mother or father may be drawn into playing that she (or he) is the baby while the child takes the role of a parent. As a variation on this theme, the small child may want to take the part of the baby. "Let's play I cry all night so you have to hold me," Vera often suggested to her mother. Vera had hit on a device that brought her comfort in several ways. She achieved the consolation of being held and rocked, which helped her to identify with the baby and to have more kindly feelings toward him. At the same time, she was testing her mother, since she was asking, "Would you love me if I were a baby who cried all the time?"

Such safety valves are all useful and frequently resorted to by a child as brothers and sisters are growing up together as well as when new babies complicate life.

Forestalling Trouble

Experienced mothers have discovered that it is usually easier to ward off quarrels than to settle them. When disagreements are worked out peaceably or circumvented, the children learn that there are better ways of solving their problems with one another than resorting to name-calling or blows.

Avoiding troubles calls for a sensitive ear and an eye alert to danger signals. Among those signals are increasingly shrill voices, extreme "silliness," aimless running around at top speed, or laughter that has ceased to be good-humored and is verging on hysteria. When children have reached that stage, they take offense at the slightest word or touch from a brother or sister. Controls have worn thin and they can no longer stop themselves.

Usually children are relieved, deep inside themselves, if an adult stops them when they are too wound up to unwind themselves. Intervening with a suggestion for a quieter kind of play, a few minutes of affectionate attention, a story or a song may ease the tension that has been building up. Television programs, if carefully selected, may be a resource, but some programs for children who are already excited may be overstimulating rather than soothing.

Watch for the trouble spots in the day's routine, when resentment between the children tends to run high. In some households trouble erupts during preparations for breakfast, especially if mother is not her cheeriest before her second cup of coffee, or father is rushing to get off to work. The less avoidable strain the children are under at that time, the less likely they are to tease one another. A minor change in procedures, such as postponing getting dressed until after breakfast, may start the day with less squabbling among the youngsters.

If the half hour before supper is a period when animosity tends to boil over, the reason is likely to be sheer fatigue, or hunger. Sometimes a before-supper glass of fruit juice or a few carrot sticks can improve dispositions. Some mothers find that the meal on the stove can get along with less attention than the children can. This is a good time to introduce a quiet activity the children can enjoy together.

Cultivating Friendliness

The effort to discover some kinds of play our small

children can enjoy together pays off, as it heightens their regard for one another as desirable playmates and like-able individuals. It is helpful to have in reserve some activities that will fill an odd moment of waiting or longer stretches of time. Colored pencils and paper, for instance, may be lifesavers for the ten minutes during which an excited three- and four-year-old are waiting to be picked up by Grandma.

In one family the small children get along quite well when they are allowed to dress up and "play wedding" or "going away for a visit" with a few of their parents' old clothes.

In another household, the four- and five-year-old are most agreeable to each other when they are allowed to cut pictures out of magazines and catalogues, albeit rather crudely, and paste them on sheets of wrapping paper saved for that purpose. When the older girl said to her mother one day, "Ginny is so crabby today. If you let us make scrapbooks, maybe she'll feel better," the mother felt that her daughter had taken a giant stride in assuming responsibility for a sister.

One point of contention between small brothers and sisters is that the younger too often loses, destroys, or misappropriates the treasures of the elder. Since these treasures often look like sheer junk, parents, too, tend to overlook their value to their owners. In the interest of promoting good feelings, we can usually arrange for each child to have some shelf, or drawer, or corner where he can keep possessions that are not to be touched without his permission. Some playthings may be for the use of all the youngsters in the family, but a favorite stuffed animal or picture book does not have to be shared.

Sometimes the best means of furthering friendliness is to arrange for occasional separations. If one of the youngsters goes to play at a friend's house, the other may have mother for himself, perhaps do something special with her, which is healing balm for jealousy.

The Value of Separation

"Whole-family activities" are not always the most desirable form of recreation. If one youngster goes on an excursion with father, even though it is only to watch boats on the river or to the playground in the park, while mother takes another for a treat suited to his age and tastes, everyone may be refreshed.

One of the by-products of separations is that they drive home a point we cannot make too emphatically: everyone is different; everyone need not do exactly the same thing. Young children close in age and constantly together may be so concerned lest one get more of whatever is being apportioned than the other does that they lose the satisfaction of being themselves or of developing an individuality of their own.

Separations also have other uses. After Bruce spent the night for the first time at his grandparents' house without his younger brother, he announced on returning home, "Next time Dickie should come along. I didn't have anyone to play with."

"Being Fair" Can Be a Booby Trap

We are so imbued with the need for "fairness" in dealing with our children that we sometimes wrongly equate it with "equal treatment" and sacrifice the opportunity to meet a need of one, lest it deprive his brother or sister of having exactly the same attention. Because of an illness, starting school, or perhaps a birthday, one child may become temporarily the center of attention. When such a situation arises, we need not feel guilty, although the others in the family may be artists at exploiting any tendencies we have in that direction.

"You stayed at the hospital all night with Amy when she broke her leg. I want you to stay with me, 'cause I had a bad dream," Amy's younger brother may complain. Some suitable assurance is surely in order, but *not* on the basis suggested by Amy's brother.

If every situation is not treated as if attention could be weighed and measured, and each child has found out that his special needs are always met, the three- to five-year-olds will less often raise the cry, "It isn't fair." Small children who have seen that "their turn will come" feel more kindly toward those with whom they must share their parents' love.

Half a Loaf Is Often Better Than None

In the interest of promoting congeniality, we can demonstrate the technique and the value of compromising. If two youngsters want different bedtime stories, and time is too short to read both, we could give them abbreviated versions so that each hears part of his favorite tale.

When one must wait his turn while his brother is on the swing, we can try to find something agreeable to occupy the child who is forced to wait. The capacity to give up part of what we want and cheerfully accept what we can get develops through practice and through finding that compromises bring more satisfaction than sulking.

Parents are laying the foundations for friendliness, too, when they build up each child's self-respect. Letting each one know he is loved and accepted as he is, and that he does not have to be a carbon copy of another member of the family to gain approval, also helps him accept his brothers and sisters.

Exhortations such as "Why can't you be like your brother?" or "If you would only try as hard as your sister" damage self-esteem and foment discord.

Not Position, But How It Is Dealt With, Counts

The relationship between children in a family is influenced, too, by the way their position in order of birth is handled. Being the eldest, youngest, or one of those in the middle may turn out to be an advantage, a disadvantage, or a mixture of both, depending on what each position means to the child and to his parents.

A strong bond, not always consciously recognized, may exist between a parent and the son or daughter who occupies the same rank in birth order as that parent did. By sheer law of averages, both parents are not apt to have been in the same position in their respective families. In the usual course of events, a mother who was, for example, a middle child may be partial to her own middle one, but that partiality is offset because the father, who was the youngest in his household, tends to favor his youngest.

In the Grady family, both Mr. and Mrs. Grady had been "youngests." When their sons were three and four and a half years old, the Gradys admitted to each other that every time the elder boy mistreated the younger one, no matter how much of a pest the younger one had been, they saw themselves as they were at an early age in their own families. They recognized their intense identification with their youngest son.

The moral of this incident is that if parents occupied comparable positions as they were growing up, they need to watch themselves lest they shortchange a particular child, or children.

Prestige and Pressure for the Eldest

The eldest has, undeniably, one advantage. His

achievements delight and astonish his parents as the attainments of subsequent offspring rarely do. Then, too, his development is not compared to that of those who have preceded him, as is inevitably the case with the others. The magic and the legends surrounding the firstborn from time immemorial attest to how important the eldest is to his parents.

The eldest usually lords it over the younger ones and usually receives from them, much of the time, an admiration that can be a tonic to his spirits. If the eldest is a boy, with younger sisters, he is looked up to as he may never be again in his lifetime.

Yet, a firstborn pays dearly for his prestige. His parents' pride in him is matched by their lack of experience. "We learned more from our first child than he learned from us," parents often say. "When I think of all we expected from our eldest and the responsibilities we gave him, well, I can only marvel that he turned out as well as he did," a mother admits.

The "Only Child" Hangover

A study carried on by J. B. Gilmore and Edward Zigler, to determine how birth order was tied up with a need for approval or reward, found that eldest children were more dependent on encouragement and praise from others when they were under stress than were later children in the families studied. The investigators suggest that perhaps eldests, who were "only children" in their earliest years, became accustomed to emotional support from their parents and are therefore frustrated when such support is absent.

Because so much is expected of him, and because,

too, he is likely to have a certain prejudice against babies and their ways, the eldest in a family may be old and serious beyond his years.

"Seniority rights" granted him help to compensate for drawbacks his position brings with it. Staying up later than his juniors, being allowed somewhat more freedom to go about on his own when he is four and a half or five, may seem like small matters, but they are cherished privileges.

At least, the eldest need not be held down to the level of the younger ones because of convenience. "Linda can wait to start nursery school until her brother is old enough to go." "Linda is really too old for a nap, but I make her take one anyway because her brother still needs one." Such treatment over the years, plus having little brother at her heels when she played with other children, made Linda resentful of him. Being kept to routines and activities suited to a child a year and a half her junior also interfered with her development.

Allowing for slight differences in age as well as for diversity of tastes and temperaments may seem to complicate the parents' task for the moment, but the basic difference between a family and an institution is that a family can, most of the time, provide for the special requirements of each of its members. Such provision is a good setting for healthy development.

Being in the Middle

Proverbially, the middle child—or children in the middle—are thought to be at a disadvantage, not sure where they belong, likely to get lost in the shuffle. This widespread notion is far from accurate. Being the one in the middle is what the child and his parents make of it. The mental picture the boy or girl forms of his situation, based on how he is treated and what he hears, makes it favorable or unfavorable. Actually, more latitude is inherent in this position than in being in the better-defined spot of eldest or youngest.

If a middle child feels neglected, as Pauline did, she will strive for attention by fair means or foul. Pauline had more than her share of problems but not more than her share of anything else. That sad state of affairs was not the result of her position in birth order in itself. Her own nature and some unhappy circumstances in the family during her early years were, in combination, stronger influences than being the second of three children.

Burt, another middle child, fairly reveled in the distinction he was given by being the only one who had both an elder and a younger brother. By the time he was five, he had figured out that he could get the privileges of seniority that the eldest enjoyed. At the same time he could join forces with his three-year-old brother when that suited his purpose. He was an aggressive boy with a positive talent for landing on his feet. Perhaps because he was impelled, without being aware of it, to make an extra effort to win affection, or because he was by nature friendly and full of fun, he went out of his way, even at an early age, to be agreeable. None of the legendary burdens of the middle child weighed on him!

Special Privileges

Parents may need to be imaginative in finding ways

to let a middle child be special or get recognition. In one family, the middle girl was occasionally permitted to do something that symbolized being "big" before her older brother had done it. She was the first in the family to go to her grandparents' home in another city for a week's visit. Her mother also built up in her a proud feeling of being "special" because she was the only girl in the family.

If need be, distinction can come for the middle child through being the only son or only daughter, "being the only one who has red-gold hair like great-grandmother Flannery had," or "being the one with a smile like her Daddy's." This needs to be handled carefully, however, so that the child does not feel it is his only reason for being loved or his only claim to distinction.

A hazard for the middle one of three is that the oldest and the youngest may ally themselves, which frequently happens. Then the middle one is, at best, left out. At worst, he or she becomes the butt of the teasing of the two others.

Mothers and fathers can take care, too, that in protecting the youngest from the tricks of the elder ones they do not leave the middle one defenseless. One middle child, looking back, says he was always punished if he attacked his small brothers, but his parents did nothing to protect him from his domineering older sister and the havoc his younger brothers too often made of his toys and projects. Although his memories of the wrongs done him were doubtless exaggerated, his parents probably did not guard his rights as carefully as they might have.

Does It Pay to Be Youngest?

The very circumstances that may hamper the older ones in a family often work to the advantage of the youngest. Parents are more relaxed, more experienced, and not in such a hurry to see this youngster grow up. The youngest never suffers displacement and has plenty of time to finish the business of being a baby. He is often given great affection and indulged in a manner the others may never have enjoyed. A father relates:

When our youngest was born we knew we were capable of being reasonably good parents. Both my wife and I were scared when our first child was small. We were so uptight about everything, from the way we held her to our fear that she wouldn't measure up in some way, that we hardly had any fun with her. Our youngest was a "good baby" and has been easy to live with these three years. Maybe we are easier to live with and so he's more self-confident than his sister ever was.

A mother says:

The advantage the youngest in our family has had is that we have more perspective on life, a better idea of what's important and what isn't. We don't feel it's the end of the world if we have to cancel an evening's plans because he's sick and we don't want to leave him with the usual teen-age sitter. I've learned that a three-and-a-half-year-old's tall tales aren't "lies," and that if he takes something that isn't his he's not "stealing."

"The best thing that happens to the youngest, from what I've seen," reports another parent, "is that they've got the older ones not just to play with and to defend them in the neighborhood, but to be models for them and to learn from. Youngest children seem to be more mature. Our younger girl is more mature at four than her older sister was at six."

Boons of a Large Family

A final advantage a youngest often benefits from in a large family is that he finds among the older children, perhaps in the eldest, one who forms a special attachment for him and to whom he is especially attached. That one may become his protector, his mentor, and his ideal—almost like another mother or father, but not as remote as a parent is likely to be.

On the debit side for the youngest is the fact that although parents may be wiser than they were, they are also older. If they have had several children, they may be a bit weary of the duties parenthood imposes. Being five or ten years older than they were when the first child was small, engaging in a rousing game of hide-and-seek or roughhousing with a vigorous four-year-old may be less fun than it was. Parents' meetings at nursery school or kindergarten, even the spring picnic for parents and children, may be a too-oft-repeated scene to be interesting.

One who is far younger than the other children in the family may be either dragged unwillingly or left behind when vacations or excursions are planned chiefly with the older children in mind. If most of the conversation in the family is over the head of the youngest,

and if his efforts to take part in it are continually be-
littled, he may feel, although he would not phrase it
that way, that he is stuck in a backwater and cannot
get into the mainstream of family life.

Plaints of "Youngests"

Jane was such a youngster. She had often heard
conversation about "the wonderful time we had the
summer before Jane was born." Her complaint was,
"You had all the fun before you had me, and you used
it all up. It isn't fair."

Another accusation some youngest children make
is that they have "too many bosses." Indeed, one of the
disguises, and a thin one at that, for hostility on the
part of the elder brothers or sisters is bossiness toward
their juniors.

The parents of a five-year-old girl who was constantly correcting, criticizing, and interfering with her
three-year-old brother were worried about her behavior.
They were aware that the boy was becoming at once
too dependent on his sister and too angry at her for his
own good.

"She means well, but about one tenth of her bossiness would be enough," the mother said when she was
discussing the problem with her husband.

"Who says she means well?" the father demanded
indignantly. He had had an older sister to contend with
and on that account was not too charitable toward his
daughter. "She's just trying to show us how superior
she is to her brother. She's such a newcomer to halfway
decent behavior herself that she has to keep proving to
herself and to us that she knows what's right. If you

ask me, she's getting to be a self-righteous little prig."

When his wife asked him what he proposed to do about their daughter, he said, "If she needs to boss something, we'll get her a kitten. That's what my mother did when my sister was driving me up the wall, and it was a good idea, too. She won't warp the kitten's personality, and maybe she'll let her brother alone for a while."

Children Learn from Each Other

In the daily interchanges between the children in the family, each is constantly learning from the others. Much as the skills and information they acquire in this way contribute toward their development, perhaps what they discover about the feelings of others and about their own feelings is even more valuable.

They can absorb, in small doses, an understanding of the principle that is so essential for emotional well-being: that it is possible to be angry at those one loves and to recover from that anger. They discover, too, that someone else's wrath may descend on you when you are quite innocent, but that you will survive without losing either self-respect or status. They are likely to accept more readily the fact that nobody can have the exclusive love and full-time attention of another human being, if they learn that lesson in the relatively protected setting of the family.

Another enduring truth that is usually instilled through the rough-and-tumble of brotherly and sisterly rivalry, if it exists in a not overwhelmingly intense degree, is that although nobody gives you the complete protection you sometimes would like to have, and everyone at times falls short of the trust you have placed in him, both protection and trustworthiness will probably be available from members of your family when you most need them.

Because moments of mutual affection come and go, in others and within oneself, the part-time absence of affection does not mean a lack of basic regard for those others nor does it weaken the potential for compatibility with them.

These are among the lessons that are taught, without anybody putting them into words, as the children in a family grow up with both love and friction as their daily fare.

"Only" Need Not Equal "Lonely"

The absence of opportunities for that kind of emotional learning is a disadvantage for the only child. The stereotype that he is selfish and spoiled is too often inaccurate as far as selfishness with material things is concerned. The necessity for sharing attention is harder for him to accept. The "spoiling" an only child may suffer from is likely to be an interference with his drive to do for himself. His capacity to be independent may be "spoiled," or at least the development of that capacity may be slowed down. When there is only one child in the family, parents may give him more protection than he needs or can profit from. The mother of an only son says:

My husband and I magnified everything our boy did, both the good behavior and the bad. We never learned to be casual, and he didn't either. I think he took us too seriously. If there had been other children, he would have discovered that I'm likely to get very impatient when anyone is slow. He wouldn't have felt I was just disappointed in him and that he was "bad." He probably would have figured out, "Mom treats everybody like that."

In discussing the only child in his book *The Child, The Family and the Outside World*, Dr. D. W. Winnicott, a British psychiatrist, says:

For all children, the big difficulty is the legitimate expression of hate, and the only child's relative lack of opportunity for expressing the aggressive side of his nature is a serious thing. Children who grow up together play games of all kinds, and so have a chance to come to terms with their own aggressiveness, and they have a valuable opportunity for discovering on their own that they mind when they really hurt someone they love.

"Only" Can Be "Different"

Another disadvantage of the only child is that he tends to be so much in the company of adults and is so eager to have their approval that he finds it hard to enter into the play and the conspiracies of his contemporaries. He does not know how to make common cause with them. He is likely to be serious and overconscientious, and as a result of his anxiety over doing wrong he may be somewhat timid.

Looking back on herself at the age of five, one woman relates:

I only had to open my mouth for the other children to know I was in some way different. I used such big words! I wanted to play with the other children on the block, but at the same time they frightened me. I was so much more dependent on my parents' approval than they were. I couldn't have described the difference between me and my friends who had sisters and brothers, then, but what it amounted to was that if they were out of favor with their parents, they still had each other. If my parents were to get angry with me, which seldom happened, I was absolutely alone.

Many sound reasons for having only one child exist today. The youngster in that position does have the advantage of having his parents for himself. Not being required to share them at an early age gives his world a degree of stability and reinforces his trust in mother and father, who, after all, have not betrayed him by having another baby. That trust in his parents often facilitates his establishing trust in other people, too.

Substitute Siblings

Fortunately, parents can, to a great extent, fill in the lack of relationships with other children. Nursery school and play groups give an "only" a chance to be with others on a close and continuing basis. Cousins are almost a substitute for brothers and sisters for some only children. When family outings are planned, an only child can be encouraged to invite a friend to go along. Visits back and forth in the homes of other children, to spend the day or night, are a treat to the four- and five-year-olds.

These visits can be brief at first. An "only" may need his mother's presence in order to feel comfortable the first time he visits in a home strange to him. Not every visit will be a great success, but the discovery that on some days other children are agreeable and on other days they are less so is a vital one, too.

One of the benefits an only child reaps is that he learns to play by himself and to develop resources for being happily occupied. "Onlies" often have a rich imaginative life and may become more creative as a result.

A youngster may not be the only child in the family and yet be in the position of being "only." One girl in a large family of boys, one boy with a number of sisters, children widely separated in age, or a child who is markedly different from the others in the household may have the same needs for companionship with children outside the family as the one who is without brothers or sisters.

No child encounters all the forms of competition or affection that it is possible for preschoolers to be exposed to. No child experiences all the advantages or disadvantages that can come from his position in the family. Rarely is a youngster steadily drawn to or repelled by any one of his sisters or brothers. The ebb and flow, the variation in direction of those currents of affection and resentment, which exist side by side and often intermingle, give richness and flavor to the daily life of brothers and sisters and stimulate their growth in many directions.

3

Helping Your Child Get Along With Others

A<small>N EARNEST YOUNG</small> father brought his three-year-old to nursery school on opening day and remained to watch him for a few minutes. The boy stayed next to his father for a moment or two and then began tentatively to explore the room. He sat down at a table where puzzles were laid out, looked at the girl sitting next to him, fitted three or four pieces of the puzzle together, and moved on to explore the block corner. Here he stopped again, said something to another child, saw the toy fire engine in the middle of the floor, and made straight for it. He played with that briefly, then left it to watch two children kneading play dough at another table.

One of the volunteer assistants came up to the father and said, "Jeff seems fine. You don't have to stay, though of course you are welcome to."

"I'd like to stay until I see him making friends and cooperating," was the reply.

"In that case you may be around quite a while. The threes aren't up to much cooperation, and we don't hurry them into it. As for making friends, it looks to me as if Jeff is off to a good start."

Developing Sociability

This father is not unusual. Most parents, in their eagerness to have their children make friends and function well in a group, tend to be impatient with the slowness of the process. Sociability is an important facet of development, but it takes years to flower.

How can we expect threes, fours, and fives to behave with one another?

How can we help them learn to balance sharing and standing up for their own rights?

What about those who are too shy or are troublemakers?

How much and what kind of supervision do children need from adults as they play together in their own neighborhood?

Small children need to find out how to get along with grown persons outside the family, too, and that brings up the question of manners. Is there a place for good manners today?

Shall we send our children to nursery school, and if so, when? How shall we choose a nursery school?

Playmates Contribute to Growth

Playing with other children in the neighborhood, going back and forth between homes, contributes in vital ways to a child's development. Playmates are, first of all, fun. They also educate one another, although sometimes it may seem to parents that what their son or daughter learns from other children in the way of vocabulary or manners leaves much to be desired.

Growth in the ability to get along with others is one of the important directions in which children need to reach out during the preschool years. If the skills of cooperation and compromise are acquired before a boy or girl enters first grade, this will make his life in school easier.

As children play together, they gain practice in solving problems, taking in fresh ideas, responding flexibly to unfamiliar situations. They grow in all directions, sharpening their wits on one another's plans and supplementing one another's imaginative flights of fancy. Play is a child's way of learning and is important preparation for formal education. A child who misses out on the companionship of other children during these years is losing the chance to make the most of his potential for learning.

Tolerance Is an Individual Matter

Different children are ready at different ages for varying amounts of the society of their contemporaries. Some preschoolers will be at a more immature level of companionship than their age mates—which suits them. Youngsters will differ, too, in the length of time each can sustain the effort of being peaceably in the company of other children; and it often is an effort, as well as pleasure.

Some children will play with friends for two or

three successive days and then want to stay at home and be near mother for a day or two. Others are always ready for companionship.

When you suggest to another mother that her son or daughter come to play with yours, you need not feel slighted if she says this is one of those days when her child wants to "stay home with Mommy."

Mothers have their own needs for being with others and being alone. Sometimes, too, they are too overwhelmed with other responsibilities to get their child together with another youngster. When that occurs, nobody need feel deficient. "Honestly, I just can't, because . . ." followed by a recital of obligations and tasks is not a brush-off when you hear it from a friend or a woman you would like to have for a friend, nor is it a lame excuse when you resort to it yourself.

Parents may grow weary of being reminded of the tremendous variation in the ability to get along with others that children manifest. Yet it is only human nature to feel, "Why is Tina so quarrelsome when other children seem to play together without fights?" or "What's the use of taking Bobby to play with another little boy? After half an hour he either goes wild or wants to go home. Then the other kid and his mother are disgusted."

The reasons Tina or Bobby or anyone else cannot hold up as well as his or her contemporaries may be unrelated to sociability. Other events in the child's life, or his rapid growth in other directions at this particular time, may be draining off so much energy that extended periods of play with other children may be more than he can handle.

Mothers can save themselves trouble if they accept the needs and tastes of the threes, fours, and fives in companionship. If a child and the son or daughter of the mother's best friend or closest neighbor are at their worst in each other's presence, that is no reflection on the child or the mother. Two months or three years from now these children may get along beautifully if they are not forced to play together now.

Stages in Friendliness

To understand the response of one preschool child to another, it may be useful to glance at the early development of awareness of others the same size. Anna Freud describes several stages in the unfolding of sociability. A baby looks on any other baby who comes between him and his mother as a disturbance. If his mother cuddles another baby, the year-old or eighteen-month-old child expresses his rage in no uncertain terms.

In the next stage, which usually comes about in the second year, one child will be interested in another as he might be attracted by a piece of furniture or a teddy bear. His treatment of the other toddler is about what his treatment of any object would be. He pushes, prods, possibly bites or kisses him, but has no interest in him as a person.

To a two-year-old, another his own size becomes interesting, but usually more for some particular feature than as an entity. A small girl with long, bright red hair came to play with another two-year-old who had never seen hair that color on someone his own size. He wanted to stroke it and gave it a few pulls. These were in the nature of exploration, not an attack.

Two- to three-year-olds play alongside each other but seldom really interact. They may use the same toy, but in different ways. One such toddler was having a lovely time putting empty spools into a basket, and another, seated by his side, was equally preoccupied in taking them out, but this was not a game they were playing together. Children of this age may be playing at opposite sides of a room. If you watch them carefully, you will see that they are observing each other and really have an awareness of being together.

Even three-year-olds often carry on "conversations" in which each pursues his own line of thought, but there seems to be no relation between the two lines, nor do the topics ever merge.

In *The Conditions of Human Growth*, Jane Pearce and Saul Newton say:

It might be useful for a little cooperation on the part of the child with other children to be enforced—taking turns, sharing, accepting retaliation for injuries inflicted on others. It is a misconception, however, to think that the child will like this. The child cooperates easily with friendly adults, but pushing him too hard to cooperate with contemporaries tends to set up resistance to the natural development of cooperation.

Of course, stages in friendliness overlap and do not occur at a precise age, but somewhere around the age of three and a half, give or take a few months, a youngster will be interested in having the help of another to carry out a project.

"I'm building a spaceship. Want to help, Mike?" says Steve.

"O.K. I'll put this big block back here and it'll be the part we leave on the moon." Mike entered into the spirit of the construction with ideas of his own, but when Steve and Mike lost interest in the spaceship they also lost interest in each other for the remainder of the morning.

Some four-year-olds and most five-year-olds have real friendships at times, as well as still valuing another child solely as one who is useful in furthering a project. In the friendship stage of the fours and fives, other children are liked and disliked, competed with and admired, imitated and hated by turns. Perhaps the test of real regard on the part of one for another is whether one misses the other when they are separated.

New Ideas from Playmates

Whether they be friends, playmates, or just playing side by side, indoors or out, small children in the course of an hour or two are likely to want the same toy, tricycle, or wagon at the same moment. When a group of children were playing in front of the apartment house where most of them lived, Paul grabbed a wagon belonging to one of the group, pulled it around, and declared, "I'm the man selling ice-cream bars. Who wants ice-cream bars?"

Suddenly, the wagon, unused for half an hour, became desirable to everyone. Another child demanded a turn at it, and still another child tried to grab it from Paul.

Such action was not sheer perversity. Children

learn from imitating one another as they play. The behavior of one may stimulate similar play in another. He takes over, elaborates, or transforms being an ice-cream-bar man into being, perhaps, the man who brings a load of furniture or a fireman putting out a fire. Imitating a type of activity, but not the exact activity itself, is referred to by child development professionals as "modeling."

Models may precipitate desirable behavior as often as more dubious kinds. Often we speak of the "contagion" of the behavior of a model when one child indulges in wild aggressiveness and others also become truculent, though in different ways.

In the demand of other children for the wagon, one shouted, "Hey, that's not an ice-cream wagon. It's a fire engine, you jerk, you, Paul! Let me have it."

This five-year-old would-be fireman seldom ventured into play that required his taking on the role of an adult. One interesting facet of "modeling" is that an action or type of play not usual for a child may be called forth by what the model does.

Like many disputes, this one was settled without adult interference. Gail, Paul's five-year-old sister, stepped in, somewhat self-righteously. "You can't have that wagon yet. You wait until Paul is through with it. Don't you know about taking turns?"

Gail was a child who identified with the feelings of others. She was able, frequently though not invariably, to put herself in someone else's shoes. She could take on another's feelings, understand his aims, as she was doing now in entering into Paul's pleasure in his role of ice-cream vendor. Human motives are complex.

Gail's championing of her younger brother, which the others accepted, also fitted in with her fondness for telling other children what to do. Gail was a leader, but a leader who could both take account of another's needs and derive satisfaction from running things.

Teaching Sharing

Gail had the background that helps children become fairly willing sharers. Her parents were cheerful, warm, friendly people. Gail's mother had not demanded that her children share their most cherished toys. When another child was coming to play with Gail, her mother would suggest that a favorite doll or stuffed kitten "take a rest for this afternoon," and would put these out of sight. This mother also kept in reserve for such occasions one or two "sharing toys" that could be used by two or three children playing together.

Gail's mother was not aware that some rather impressive research studies have pointed out that youngsters who spend their early years in a lenient, loving atmosphere, in which children are treated as individuals likely to do what is expected of them, tend to be more accepting of others and to cooperate with them better than those who grow up in a family in which conformity is sternly enforced and any deviation from strict regulations is a serious misdemeanor. The way the members of a family treat one another carries over in some degree to the way young children treat their playmates.

Learning Takes Time

Children need time and practice to learn generous

behavior. If the wait for one's turn is not too long, and if sharing brings outspoken approval from adults and from other children, gradually, although steadily, over months and years, the preschooler discovers that waiting is worth the effort. Some of the face-saving compromises discussed in the previous chapter are equally useful when children are playing with friends.

Four- and five-year-olds tend to respond to such phrases as, "She *needs* the dress-up hat now, but she will be through with it soon," or "He is *using* the car now." The child who has the desired object may relinquish it more readily if the request from an adult who has stepped in is phrased in words that have meaning to him, for instance, "When will you be through with it?" Learning to share is less painful to the young if they have a chance to carry out a line of thought before the toy they need for it has to be relinquished. "It would help if you would let me have the boat now, because he is a fisherman who must catch fish for his dinner," or "You *might* give her a turn on the swing now," are also approaches that make it easier, sometimes, to be generous.

Generosity tends to be contagious. Children who have been watching a child who behaves generously are more likely to be generous themselves afterward. Exposure to an ungenerous model has the effect of producing unwillingness to share, experiments have shown.

No phrase, example, or interpretation works magic, but some approaches do tend to impress on small boys and girls the idea that taking turns and sharing are necessary.

In spite of our best efforts to make clear to a

three-year-old that generosity does not mean, "What's yours is mine, and what's mine remains mine," we may discover a misconception in the mind of our offspring, as Doug's mother did. Doug and a friend were drinking lemonade. Doug, having finished his own, leaned over and began sucking on one of the straws in his friend's glass. In outraged tones, Doug's mother said, "Whatever in the world are you doing, Doug?" "I'm sharing his lemonade," was that young man's bland answer.

Stumbling Blocks to Friendliness

Many children are not as aggressive or as confident as Doug. They are shy and find standing up for their own rights difficult. Overcoming shyness and discovering how and when to assert oneself are also learnings that come about slowly with practice. Almost every child is shy at times. Indeed, the three-year-old who stands, thumb in mouth, at the edge of a noisy group of strange children at a birthday party or in the park, or who refuses to stay without his mother at the home of another child, is not unduly shy. Such behavior is to be expected at three.

A five-year-old who cannot be comfortable with two or three children, even though he has been with them frequently, is exhibiting a different order of shyness and needs help from the adults around him. Perhaps he is one of those persons who will always be somewhat shy and be content to be by themselves for long stretches of time. Being a "loner" is, within limits, perfectly acceptable even in our gregarious society, but our goal for our children is to have them be at ease with others even though they are quite happy without company.

Sometimes a child who has previously been friendly and self-assured will, because of a frightening incident or for some other reason, become unwilling to leave his mother and turn extremely shy. If that happens, we may have to start over again with small doses of companionship. If there is an obvious cause for his uneasiness, such as a new baby in the family, a move to a new neighborhood, the divorce of his parents, or the death or departure of someone close to him, parents may help him if they put his anxiety into words.

"You feel sort of strange since we moved here. That always happens to people in a new place to live. You'll get used to it here. You know what? I'm getting used to it, a little more every day." Such a statement lets him know he is not alone in his trouble, but that a parent whom he relies on is still strong enough to cope.

The Need for Reassurance

One youngster who came home from play and was told by a family friend that his mother had been in an accident and had been rushed to the hospital, was afraid to leave her side when she returned a few days later. Realizing what a shock this four-year-old had undergone, the mother allowed him to stay close to her for a week or so. Then, when he was still unwilling to join his former comrades she said, "You probably think if you go out to play, I won't be here when you come back. I'll be right here. I won't go anywhere unless I tell you about it first." Repeated reassurance in words, plus acceptance of his coming in from play quite frequently to be sure his mother was where she belonged, gradually made him feel safe in joining the other children.

Sometimes the cause of unwillingness to play with other children is not so easily identified. One little girl who was always on the outskirts of a group and rarely became involved with others was discovered to have a slight hearing loss owing to repeated ear infections and enlarged adenoids. When medical procedures restored her hearing, she began to play with other children with enthusiasm. Physical problems are not often so readily resolved, but if a child is persistently unwilling or unable to enjoy the company of his contemporaries, the possibility of a physical impairment of some kind, however slight, should be checked out.

Helping to Foster Sociability

Rather than trusting that a timid boy or girl will outgrow his aversion to sociability, we can aid the forces of development by giving him opportunities to be with one child at a time for a brief interval. Two is often company and three an overwhelming crowd for the very young. A shy child may enjoy playing with another youngster if his mother's presence gives him the support he needs when he is in someone else's home, or he may be happier if a friend comes to him.

Some three- and four-year-olds play outdoors with others for a short while and then need to come in for a few minutes with mother. After a period of following her around, they are ready to venture forth again. Such behavior can be exasperating to a busy mother, especially in winter when putting on boots and snowsuits

can be a bother, but this is not a case of the youngster's not knowing what he wants. He knows very well not only what he wants, but what he needs, although he may not have the language to express it: a respite from accommodating himself to company. He may have found a sensible compromise for managing his shyness.

Parents may need to encourage some small ones who do not have the courage to stand up for their own rights: "Ask him if you may have the tricycle now," or "Tell her you need to use the doll carriage."

Suggestions of this sort are preferable to either shaming a timid child or urging him to hit back or strike a child who is not willing to give up a toy. Standing up for one's rights, even in three- to five-year-old circles, need not be synonymous with a willingness to fight.

Some children who live in unusually conflict-free or extremely repressed households may find it difficult to assert themselves. The conviction, born of experience, that one can get angry and get over it, and that making a demand is not dangerous, is necessary before one can believe one has any "rights" whatsoever.

How Skills Can Help

Researchers who have studied children's behavior tell us that boys and girls are more secure with others of their own age if they can do the things that are valued. The five-year-old who can ride a bicycle and/or throw a ball, who is acquainted with the way to manipulate clay and use paints, who is adept at rudimentary hide-and-seek, freeze tag, and similar games loved by fours and fives tends to be wanted by his fellows and therefore enjoys them and feels more confident in playing with them.

One study of nursery-school-age children showed that a boy or girl who has had experiences and possesses information he can translate into dramatic play is more likely to be acceptable to other children. For example, a child who has been to the zoo, who has watched a bulldozer or a crane being operated, who has "helped" his father do a repair job around the house or his mother bake bread, has the raw materials for playing at adult activities.

Children who have grown up in a restrictive, repressive atmosphere are less likely to exhibit imagination, zest, and spontaneity in play. They are apt to be dismissed as "no fun to play with." That is often really a valid pronouncement. The vicious circle of a child's being shy because he is not well liked, being rejected because he offers little, and not being imaginative or full of ideas because he has been repressed at home needs to be broken before he can become more assertive.

Tattling Versus Responsible Reporting

A number of investigators of children's behavior with playmates have found that children who are not dependent on adults are better liked. The child who frequently turns from his play to seek reassurance from grown persons is less in demand. The one who asks a grown person for help in an activity or in something he is making is a different matter. Such requests do not prejudice his peers against him.

The "emotional dependence" that these studies investigated includes behavior that in everyday language would be called tattling. Young children are apt to carry tales for a number of reasons. Parents need to distinguish between responsible reporting of a dangerous situation and officious tale-bearing. If a five-year-old or a four-year-old comes in the house to tell us breathlessly that another youngster has climbed on the roof of a shed and cannot get down, or that one of the three-year-olds is pedaling his small automobile in the road, that is a sensible and responsible act. Since we never know what we may hear, we should listen to what our son or daughter has to tell before we launch into a tirade against tattling.

If we are treated to an unnecessary and priggish recital of the minor wrongdoings of one of the neighborhood children, as Lynn's parents frequently were, we can always say something like "Now really, that isn't any of our business, is it?"

Lynn's mother was aware that a desire to get another child into trouble was not the motive for her daughter's tales. Lynn had so recently, and so waveringly, established her own resistance to the very temptations she related others as having succumbed to, that she needed to reassure herself and her mother that she knew better than to fall into such ways!

Being an informer is so distasteful a role to most of us that we are likely to feel disgraced if our own child seems eager to make trouble for someone else. Yet, for the three- to five-year-old, tale-bearing is more a way of reinforcing his own controls than of acting maliciously, as an older child might be doing by tattling.

An instructive contrast between our values and those taught Russian children comes out in *Two Worlds of Childhood: U.S. and U.S.S.R.* by Urie Bronfenbrenner. From the time they enter any group, children in the Soviet Union are taught to "evaluate" the behavior of their friends and dispense criticism or praise as their judgment may dictate. To us, who are steeped in the "mind your own business" tradition, this procedure would seem to encourage exactly what we discourage as "tale-bearing."

Bullies Need Help

Some children seek to display their power and attain their own ends by threatening or coercing weaker playmates. Even bullies aged three, four, and five sense whom they can dominate and whom it is useless to threaten. Usually the bully is an unhappy, insecure child who uses his blustering to cover up his own fear. George was such a four-and-a-half-year-old. All that he had seen in the behavior of his brothers and his parents had led him to conclude that bullying was just about the only way of communicating with others. George saw the world as full of danger and regarded himself as unprotected and not worthy of protection.

The father of a boy whom George had been threatening and pushing around was a man of exceptional sympathy and humanity. Instead of scolding George or sending him home when he appeared, he tried being kind to him and showing an interest in him. When this man took his two boys on an after-supper bicycle ride on a summer evening, he would invite George, who was standing sullenly in his own doorway, to join them.

When another neighbor praised this man for his altruism, his answer was, "If we're going to live on this street, it better be a place where my children can play without being scared to death. The most constructive thing I can do is to try to get to George. I think there's hope for him if we don't all expect him to live up to his reputation of being a terror."

Adults outside a child's family can often help a small bully toward better ways of dealing with others and toward a better opinion of himself, too.

The child who habitually bites, hits, kicks, or pulls hair may need more than a kindly adult to trust before he can handle his feelings acceptably. In the one- or two-year-old, hitting, hair-pulling, and biting can be expected to occur occasionally. If the three- to five-year-old child habitually resorts to such acts and has no other means of solving his problems, professional counseling may be needed, but various kinds of "emotional first aid" are worth trying first.

Helping Ease Hidden Fears

Such a child is afraid of many things, but perhaps most of all his own impulses to violence. Deep inside himself he wants to be stopped when he attacks someone. He needs protection from himself, not punishment, by removing him from other children. As a seasoned nursery school teacher said, "When you hurt other people, you need to be by yourself for a bit, until you can manage not to hurt others. I don't let anyone hurt you, and I won't let you hurt anyone. People don't like to be hurt. Next time you can find a better way to get what you want."

Pointing out some better ways, such as asking for what he wants or seeking help from an adult, may be helpful to him.

When a child needs to be restrained from going after another, you can hold him, as gently as it is possible to hold an angry youngster, and say as calmly as you can, "I can't let you do that. I take good care of you."

Building up a child's own picture of himself as someone capable of "finding better ways" is useful, too, but if such emotional first-aid steps are ineffective, then his trouble may go deeper. Help from a child guidance clinic or family counselor may be called for. Seeking such help is not an admission of failure on the part of a parent, and securing it promptly may save the child and his family, not to mention the victims of his attacks, from suffering.

The family doctor or clinic, the minister, priest, or rabbi, the Family Service Society, Mental Health Association, or Child Care Society are among the resources available to locate the guidance clinic, social agency, or child therapist in private practice who can help a child. In a metropolitan area, the telephone listings may be under "Community Referral Service" or "Welfare Council." These agencies know the qualified professional municipal or state clinics as well as the private organizations in the area.

Finding Playmates

For some families, the question is not whether a young child plays well with others, but how to find others near his age for him to play with. If parents are newcomers in the neighborhood or for some reason hesitate to make advances, playmates may be harder to come by.

The happiest situation usually exists when neighborhood children have only to go outdoors and other youngsters appear on the sidewalk or in the backyard. Not all the neighborhood companions may be equally desirable. In friendships between the very young there are sure to be low points. Feelings will be hurt, from time to time, but availability makes up for a multitude of shortcomings.

Mothers enjoy sociability, too, and taking a small child to play with a son or daughter of a friend who may live several miles away provides company for both generations. When this is done, the mother should keep in mind that the host-guest relationship between small children need not duplicate that which good manners dictates for those who are twenty years older.

If a family is new to the neighborhood and no playmates seem to be visible, taking the children to the nearest park or playground may produce at least "playground friends" for them. Overtures to other mothers, if the children seem congenial, may lead to an exchange of home visits, too.

Parents often find, in a new community, that membership in a church, attendance at P-TA meetings (if there are older children in the family), or participation in some activity with like-minded neighbors leads to finding playmates for the preschoolers.

Nursery School or Alternatives

Enrolling a three- or four-year-old in a good nursery school, of course, assures him companionship. If that is not practicable, an arrangement such as made by Mrs. Anson and two of her friends might be suitable. The three families lived a mile or two apart in an area where preschool company was all but nonexistent. Each of them took the three children for one morning a week. One mother would pick up one child and deposit him, along with her own, at the home of the woman who was caretaker for the day. This was a firm commitment. The children became accustomed to one another as playmates and to the mothers as reliable and kindly overseers of their play. Each mother agreed to have some materials ready for the children to use or some activity planned for at least part of the morning, and to take time to read a story or play a record or two for the children. In pleasant weather the children played outdoors or went for a walk with the supervising mother. It was agreed that the children would not watch television nor be dragged around on a mother's shopping trips. The plan worked well for the winter before these four-year-olds entered kindergarten. Sometimes, if one child was sick, only two would be together.

Children who play together without undue quarreling, who do not frequently overexcite, overtire, or threaten one another, can be "desirable" playmates no matter what their background. Young children tend to absorb their parents' views and values as to what makes somebody "nice to play with" or "not nice to play with." The more kinds of children a boy or girl gets to know and feel comfortable with, provided they are agreeable companions and play constructively most of the time, the richer his experiences will be and the more easily he will fit into the larger society as he grows up.

Supervising Play

Whenever the three- to five-year-olds play together, a grown person or a responsible older child needs to keep an eye on them. A delicate balance between supervision and interference is called for.

The danger signals of mounting tension and some ways of coping with them were described in the preceding chapter.

Mothers may be interested in the results of research on play. When play space is restricted, conflicts tend to be more numerous. Some play materials and equipment tend to promote cooperation, among them wagons, tricycles, swings, and housekeeping materials. Clay tends to produce friendliness, but that old standby, sand, tends to induce quarreling. Children's tastes change rapidly. What appeared to be an almost ideal occupation for twos, threes, or fours last month may lead to disputes a few months later.

Some children behave in more mature fashion when they are not in their own homes; others, who still need a parent's visible presence to keep their consciences in working order, are more likely to go out of bounds away from home, especially when fatigue sets in. A responsible person needs to keep an ear to the ground for "early warning" that trouble is brewing and step in with a suggestion for a switch in activities.

For sheer safety, young children who are playing outdoors need to be checked on frequently. We never know when a three-year-old will be exhilarated by sitting in a puddle of water on a chill November day. Four-year-olds may decide it would be a good joke to hide under a pile of neatly raked leaves at the curb. No driver could possibly suspect their presence under such a mound, and the outcome could be fatal.

The way mothers, grandmothers, older boys and girls, and others in the household treat the child and his playmates may influence his standing with his friends. If a mother is welcoming, even though she is quietly and consistently firm, visiting preschoolers are apt to be comfortable. If adults are clearly annoyed at the presence of an extra child or two in the house, are capricious, yell at the children, or reprimand their own offspring severely in front of his friends, young visitors may not return or even wish to play with the son or daughter of such a house.

Supervising the play of the three-to-fives also includes protecting them and their guests when necessary from the teasing of older brothers and sisters.

Do It My Way—Nicely

The example of hospitality we set lets our children know how one should treat visitors, but hospitality can be tried beyond all reasonable limits. When those limits are exceeded by small guests, supervising mothers can enforce restrictions without being angry. Four- and five-year-old children of neighbors who arrive at breakfast time, or who ring the doorbell a dozen times a day to know if our youngster is home after having been told he is gone for the day, can be pests.

Yet, if the pests are good companions for our children and are available playmates, they may be worth tolerating. Definite rules such as, "Trudie isn't ready to go out and play before nine o'clock in the morning, so don't come over before then," or "In this house you wait until I tell you it's snack time before you go exploring in the cookie jar," can protect you and still not jeopardize friendships. Mothers need not be imposed upon by the repeated suggestion that "I *could* stay for lunch. My Mom wouldn't care."

Every neighborhood has a few children who try the patience of their playmates' mothers. When we must send such a child home, we should try to do it with tact and good nature, for congenial comrades for our children are an asset not to be disposed of lightly.

Enjoyment of Playing Alone Is Valuable

The ability to be contentedly and constructively

occupied when alone is also worth cultivating. A person who does not need constant company and/or entertainment will be saved from boredom and loneliness many times in the course of his life.

Mothers can foster the capacity to play alone by keeping on hand for their children some materials that can be enjoyed without playmates. Simple puzzles, paper and crayons, blunt scissors and old magazines or catalogues to cut up, together with large sheets of paper and paste, peg boards of all varieties, fit-together toys, and of course dolls, stuffed animals, and building equipment are among the items that lend themselves to solitary play. Not to be overlooked are albums of family snapshots or a broken clock or camera the five-year-old can take apart. Of course, no household needs to have all these resources.

Mothers may need to make suggestions and bring out materials to get a small child started playing. Until a youngster grows accustomed to playing alone, we should be satisfied if he is busy and happy for a short while. A family room, where a child can play while his mother sews or irons or his father repairs fishing tackle or reads, is a boon; playing independently need not be synonymous with being banished from human contact. It may be useful to say to a young child, "I'm going to be busy for a while, so you give your doll a bath (or whatever the suggestion may be) and then you and I will go to the store." If intervals of playing alone are followed by an enjoyable activity that a child can anticipate, he is more likely to be content, even though he may ask a few times, "Are we going to the store soon?"

It is often tempting to let the television set substitute for creative play when a child is alone. If a suitable program is to be found and the preschooler's viewing is sensibly rationed, TV may tide everyone over a drab half hour. But in the development of personality, TV-viewing does not take the place of the preschooler's ability to play imaginatively and happily by himself.

Parental example also plays a part in developing a nice blend of sociability and self-sufficiency. A mother who can be agreeably occupied by herself, who has her own resources, is telling her children something important.

Manners in Today's World

Preschoolers need to be able to get along with adults outside the family as well. Knowing how to talk to grown-ups makes a child's life easier. Good manners help. They are a way of expressing consideration for the needs and feelings of others and of conveying friendliness.

A child who hears "please" and "thank you," "good morning" and "goodnight," said cheerfully, will usually enjoy using those phrases; models have a strong influence on manners. One mother, who has always been careful to introduce her daughter to anyone she meets when the little girl is with her, was both surprised and delighted to hear the girl say, when she brought a playmate into the house and her grandmother was present, "Grandma, here is Penny. We're friends. Penny, that's my gran." Afterward the mother told the little girl how pleased Grandma was to have been introduced to Penny.

Small children feel more comfortable if they have something to do when they are presented to strangers. Knowing how to shake hands and look at the person they are talking to with a smile can diminish a tendency to shyness.

Four- and five-year-olds can learn to let adults precede them through a door, or, if they cannot avoid going first, to say "Excuse me."

Three-year-olds may have difficulty in sitting through an adult meal without leaving the table on some pretext. Letting them help clear the table often makes a virtue out of what might be a breach of good manners. When young children are learning to keep their mouths closed while chewing food, not to lean on their elbows, and whatever else is emphasized in their homes, they are likely to be loudly critical of any adult who does not observe such decorum. We may find it necessary to stress that a cardinal principle of acceptable manners is not to correct others who follow different customs—a hard bit of mannerliness to absorb!

Nursery Schools

Any discussion of how a three- to five-year-old grows in sociability necessarily includes what the nursery school experience can contribute to some children. A good nursery school is not a place where everyone is expected to engage in the same activity at the same time. Dr. D. W. Winnicott, in his book *The Child, The Family and the Outside World*, nicely defines it as "an extension upward from the family, not downward from school."

The answer to the question, "Shall I send my child to nursery school?" is, "That depends on the child and the school." A youngster who has four or five friends nearby with whom he plays regularly and fairly contentedly, whose parents have the time to read to him and let him hear music and can provide him with play materials that encourage creativity, may have no need for nursery school. Nursery school usually does offer experiences the child would not have at home, including being away from his mother for a few hours a day. Some nursery schools offer a two- or three-day-a-week program that may be a gentler introduction for the three-year-old.

A parent will want to be clear about who is responsible for running any school in which a child is to be enrolled. Many good schools are managed, owned, and directed by a well-trained nursery school teacher who makes a livelihood in that way. Since hers is a private enterprise, with no board of directors or other body to aid her in setting policy, one would want to be sure of her goals for the children and what she sees her school as offering them.

Some nursery schools are cooperatives, which means that the mothers must spend a certain number of hours working in the school under the direction of a head teacher who is a professional. Parents usually make up the board of directors.

Many nursery schools are church-connected, but some that use church buildings do not have any religious program. These, like nursery schools maintained in connection with a community center, settlement house, or similar social agency, have a professional staff and possibly volunteer aid and a policy-making board.

Other Kinds of Nursery School

Universities, colleges, and high schools may maintain a nursery school as a laboratory or training center for their child-care, psychology, or domestic science students. Public school systems in some cities have a kindergarten program for four-year-olds that is quite similar to nursery school, and some schools are under the auspices of a government agency. Fees will vary depending on the sponsorship of the school, and parents are the best judges of what they can afford. One should spend a morning visiting one or more nursery schools before deciding to enroll a child. One should also find out whether a school is licensed by the local Board of Health and approved by the state agency that licenses day-care centers and nursery schools. If it is, one may be reasonably sure that it is clean, well heated, and safe and has adequate light, ventilation, and play space, indoors and out.

Fay Bauling, who has been Chairman of the Advisory Committee for Head Start in Chicago and was for many years Licensing Representative for Day Care Centers for the State of Illinois, says this about evaluating the merits of nursery schools:

A well-planned program offers the children a wide variety of options. Both active and quiet play, opportunities to do things alone or with other children should be available throughout the session. A competent teacher sets the stage so that each child gets a chance to try out a number of activities each day, to listen and to talk, and to use different kinds of materials. One of the criteria for judging a nursery school is the amount of interaction between the children and the teachers. Are teachers warm, interested and available? Do they seem to care more about the process the children go through in their play, or creative work, than about having a product that is creditable? If that is the case, never mind if the furniture is a bit battered or the toys not the newest. Nursery school should be one place free from competition and pressure.

Drill in skills or emphasis on intricate handwork is not part of the program in a good nursery school, but that does not mean that the children are not growing through their play.

Judging a School

When a parent visits, she should watch how the teachers respond if one child hits another, overturns a jar of paint, spills a glass of juice, or disrupts the story time. Is the incident handled calmly, but immediately, in a matter-of-fact way?

Those observations will give clues as to whether a particular school will provide the kind of experiences a child needs. The comments of other parents, whose judgment can be trusted and whose children have attended the school, are also helpful.

Some youngsters seem so adept at getting along with other children and being on their own that it is a surprise to find that nursery school is a strain for them. The strain may show up in fatigue before the school session is over, in unusual irritability when the youngster returns home, or in repeated requests to be allowed to stay home. Often, allowing a child to stay home for a period of time with the understanding that he may return to school whenever he feels ready to go every day, results in his showing quite plainly when he is ready. Of course, such a plan assumes that a place for him will be available when he is ready to return.

Teachers and parents need to watch for and confer about how a youngster is getting on at home and at school before deciding how to handle problems of this sort. A parent should not decide too quickly that "nursery school is not for my child," but also should not be inflexible about his going every day if matters are getting worse instead of better.

Many three- and four-year-olds enjoy nursery school but have all the companionship they can handle in the half day there. They may want to stay near mother and not play with other children the remainder of the day. That does not mean a child is not benefiting from nursery school.

Probably one of the most conspicuous ways a child changes between his third and his sixth birthdays is in his ability to get along with other children, but his development in sociability will hardly be smooth, nor will it always be "onward and upward." He needs to try out his capacity for friendliness over and over again in a variety of settings. If he discovers that playing with others calls for accommodation and compromise, but that the fun of companionship outweighs whatever one gives up to gain it, his parents can be satisfied with his development.

4

Contrariness, And All That

ONE OF THE tasks life sets for the young child is becoming domesticated: learning the rules of his world and the special regulations within his own family; finding out when and where self-assertion is good and when it is taboo; discovering at what times, in what places, and with whom compliance and conformity will be demanded, and when greater freedom of action is permissible. Such teaching is done explicitly and implicitly by parents and is often summed up in the word "discipline." Discipline covers many kinds of parental behavior, but one that it does not cover is punishment. Punishment enters the picture only when the usual ways of living together and teaching, in other words the customary discipline, seem to have become ineffective.

Given the need to become domesticated, and the contradictory feelings of the preschooler, we need to

93

consider how we can balance freedom and controls in teaching our children.

How can discipline be consistent, yet flexible, firm but still kindly?

How can we keep our teaching and the relationships of everyday living in line with those long-range goals: independence, self-esteem, and self-control?

Discipline for the Young

That youngsters want to grow up and be like the adults they admire and love cannot be stressed too often. Much of the teaching, or discipline, parents instill is absorbed by the young through the example their parents set. What parents *are* may teach more than what they say, or do to, for, or with a child.

Children's desire to imitate and identify with their parents is a mother's and father's greatest ally in guiding their young. Yet at the same time that a boy or girl wants to be like mother and father, he wants to be himself. A young child's push for independence, to be a separate individual, to try out his powers and use initiative is strong and essential for healthy development. Some of our demands may go against the grain with him. Growing up is hard and calls for compromises, spoken and unspoken, on the part of the learning generation and the generation that teaches.

Not only his feelings, but also his imperfect understanding of what we are trying to impart, make for confusion in the young child's mind as we teach him an orderly way of living. Anna Freud, in *Research at the Hampstead Child Therapy Clinic and Other Papers*, points out:

Misunderstandings arise between parents and children because kindly, well-intentioned, sensible arrangements, based on external circumstances, . . . reason and logic, are seen by the child in terms of his wishes, fantasies and fears and come out altogether differently.

To the four-year-old, the rain does not fall on the just and the unjust. If he wants to play outside, the rain is a personal insult, or he may interpret it as the result of his having done "something bad." His father's toothache becomes, "Father is cross with me. I have done something wrong."

During the preschool years, a youngster should, and most of them do, begin to outgrow this unreal view of events.

Yet during most of this period, for most children, the logical, external reasons behind their parents' teaching filters through to them blurred by their imaginings and distorted by their immaturity.

Variety in Discipline

Every family has its own style in teaching its children the conformity necessary and in showing them how to use the freedom that is permissible. Regulations and techniques of implementing them that might appear too brusque in one household might, in another, give the children the unspoken feeling, "We know where we stand and what's expected of us."

Indeed, within a family each child will probably respond differently to the same instructions. One three-year-old may be a self-starter who needs few cues to get him involved in the day's routines, whereas his brother or sister, a year older, needs to be eased into bathtime, bedtime, and even mealtime because making transitions is still hard for him.

The regulations a family emphasizes depend, too, on the available space in their home, the parents' hours of work and leisure, the safeness of the neighborhood, the size of the family, and the closeness in age of the children. One research study of the relationship of space in the home to parental strictness found that the more rooms in the living quarters of the family, the more freedom was permitted to the children.

The testimony of the father of twelve children, three of whom were preschoolers at the time, bears this out. When a friend commented on how stringent were the rules and how submissive the children in this house, the father's reply was, "With so many of us in a house that's about three rooms too small for us, we just have to run a tight ship. There isn't any room for a kid to throw his weight around, or throw anything else around either!"

When to Discard Old Rules

Another force shaping the discipline in any family is the human tendency to bring up our children much as we were brought up, whether we intend to or not. Under some circumstances this becomes a useful handing down of customs, but sometimes old rules do not make sense under present conditions. "I didn't have a two-wheel bike until I was eight. Five-year-olds aren't old enough for two-wheelers," says a mother. Five-year-olds may not have changed in the last twenty-five years,

but bicycles have, and if the cost of the bicycle or the safety of the streets is not a factor, this mother's insistence on repeating her own experience is a poor reason for denying her child a two-wheeler.

Although discipline that furthers self-reliance and self-esteem may take a variety of forms, research studies, as reported by Martin and Lois Hoffman, in *Child Development Research*, agree: reason and praise influence children toward taking responsibility for their own behavior and being cooperative in their dealings with other people. That discipline relying chiefly on love and reasonableness furthers outgoing friendliness and self-confidence in adult life is borne out by a study of college students conducted by Marvin Siegelman. His aim was to discover if there was a relationship between the personality of these students and the discipline under which they lived as young children. He found that:

> The college students who indicated a high degree of anxiety tended to recall their parents as rejecting, while those who indicated a low degree of anxiety tended to describe their parents as loving.

We are not stretching this interpretation if we infer that individuals who are continually anxious are also lacking in confidence both in themselves and in others.

Fostering Cooperation

Reasoning with a young child does not mean becoming embroiled in a long and devious argument. "I can't take you to play with Gloria. I'm too busy," is sufficient. We need not let a three-and-a-half-year-old seduce us into trying to answer such questions as "Why must you be busy?" "When will you stop being busy?" and on and on.

We may find it useful to keep certain points in mind in giving a small child directions. A simple clear-cut statement of what we want the child to do and allowing sufficient time for him to do it increases our chances of getting his cooperation. We must be sure he understands what we are telling him. Too often instructions are over a child's head.

If we watch a nursery school teacher when she is talking to children, particularly when she is trying to put a point across to an individual youngster, we will see how frequently she sits on the floor or on a low chair, faces the child, puts an arm around him, and then, when she has his attention, explains what he is to do. Mothers and fathers can hardly do that fifty times a day, but if we want to be certain to get a point across, particularly to a boy or girl who is excited or angry, it is worth taking the time to be sure he is listening. It may save everyone the wear and tear of shouting or being shouted at later.

"No" Does Not Always Mean "No"

Preschoolers, especially those at the younger end of the age scale, are often contrary. They say "No" more often than "Yes" to requests or directions. Their "No" usually reflects their struggle to become a separate entity capable of controlling themselves and their environment, rather than sheer stubbornness or "orneriness."

A group of neighbors were bemoaning, over coffee,

their preschoolers' predilection for giving a negative response.

"I've learned that 'No' may mean 'Yes,' so I just ignore it, and about half the time Babs does what I have asked her to. She seems to have to say 'No,' and once she's said it, her protest is over," said one mother.

" 'No' from my three-year-old pretty often turns out to mean 'I'd do it myself, if you'd just let me alone.' When the 'No's' get too numerous some days, I start listening to myself, and I realize that I'm giving a lot more directions than are really necessary. If I ease up, cut out some of the 'Do this,' 'Stop that,' there's less for him to say 'No' to, and I don't get so annoyed."

A third woman, who had no children of her own, dared to raise her voice. "If anyone wants to know what I think, it's my guess that the small fry come up with all these 'No's' because that's the word they hear most."

The mother of a large family spoke up: "But you can't get away from the fact that sometimes when they say 'No' they mean it, and when you have five youngsters in the house all under the age of eight, sometimes you have to meet those 'No's' head on. I belong to the school that once in a while says, 'You're going to do as I say right now.' And believe me, it works, at least in my house, it does."

"I'm sure it does work for you, but I'm not as gutsy as you are," said a quiet young woman with a conciliatory manner. "I deal with my little girl's negativism by making a game out of the whole thing and letting her get the 'No's' out of her system. If I want her to get ready to go outdoors, I say to her 'Is your Woolly Kitty going outdoors?' and she says, 'No.' Then I go through a few more ridiculous things that aren't going out, like 'Is the table going outdoors?' and she keeps on saying 'No' and laughing about it. When I finally get around to 'Is Molly going outdoors?' she says 'Yes'—almost always."

"You'd never go through all that Mickey-Mouse if you had five to deal with," said the mother of the big family.

Stability Is Reassuring

Although we have to find our own approach to discipline, some general principles do hold true. A reasonable degree of stability in the household tends to make a youngster more comfortable. His expanding horizons, increasing independence, and freedom to get around can make his world a bewildering as well as a fascinating place. Along with his growing feeling of power is an underlying, continuing feeling of being helpless and needing protection.

A pattern to the major events of the day, such as meals and bedtime, reasonable boundaries both physical and social, as well as fairly consistent responses from the important adults in his life can supply a needed stabilizing atmosphere. Such stability and predictability differ from overprotectiveness, which implies that danger lurks everywhere. They lay the foundation for the growth of a well-organized personality.

The most disturbed children are those who feel unprotected from unknown (and usually nonexistent) dangers, from temptation, and from their own frightening impulses. This point is discussed more fully in Chapter 8.

Removing Temptation

We may be able to cut down on the number of prohibitions we have to enforce by not leaving temptation in our child's way. Some objects around the house, of course, are off limits. If those are not present in abundance, a five-year-old, and even a four or a three, can learn to stay away from them. The mother who leaves a newly made strawberry meringue pie on a kitchen counter where a three-and-a-half-year-old can pull up a chair, climb up, and sink a grimy hand into it is making trouble for herself as well as her youngster.

In protecting a child from his own impulses, we can tell him we will always stop him when he cannot stop himself. It is sometimes a surprise to parents that if we have faith in ourselves, we can usually bring a child to his senses this way. Many years ago, Dr. Lawrence Kubie described in an article in *Child Study* how a father stopped a wildly excited little girl who seemed, at the moment, intent on breaking up everything in sight. This father sat down where he could look her in the eye, held her gently but firmly, and said, "There are some things I can't let you do. I won't let you hurt yourself or hurt anyone else, and I won't let you destroy things." The little girl looked at her father in surprise and quieted down, almost gratefully.

Reminded recently in a personal conversation of this anecdote, Dr. Kubie recalled that it was his own daughter whom he had quieted that way, and he added, "Letting her know you will prevent her from getting completely out of control is still a good way of handling an out-of-bounds four-year-old."

Indirectly, when we protect a child from himself

by stopping overexcited behavior, we are telling him, "You are worth protecting. I care about you." This, too, furthers that long-range aim of discipline—enhancing self-esteem.

Knowing What Is Expected Helps

Parents who follow through on enforcing the reasonable limits they have set also facilitate a child's establishing his sense of self. He learns more about who he is. He gradually acquires the feeling, though it may remain unexpressed, "I am a person who can . . ." "I am a person who wouldn't . . .", "I am a person who is expected to . . . , and I will do it." Along with these reassuring feelings go some warning ones that can be healthy, too. "I'm not big enough yet to . . . ," or "I'd better not try to . . ." Such attitudes, when a child is faced with a challenge he could not possibly meet, are the better part of wisdom. Parents have strengthened his understanding of his real capacities through the stable structure their discipline has set up.

Freedom Within a Safe Framework

Parents in discussion groups frequently ask, "It's all very well to talk about 'reasonable limits,' but how do you decide when you are holding your children down too much and when you are letting them do as they please too much?"

Steering a safe course between the two extremes involves knowing one's child and his environment. Both restriction and freedom have a place in discipline. Every child needs to learn to accommodate himself to both. Without appropriate freedom of action, a child might be so overprotected that he would not be able to use, or to develop, the capacity to take care of himself, which takes practice. Given too much freedom, he courts obvious dangers, physical or emotional.

Mrs. Rabbit, the mother of Flopsy, Mopsy, Cottontail, and Peter, in Beatrix Potter's *Tale of Peter Rabbit*, knows this. "Now my dears," said Old Mrs. Rabbit to her brood, "you may go into the fields or down the lane, but don't go into Mr. McGregor's garden. Your father had an accident there. He was put into a pie by Mrs. McGregor."

Here we have a model of balance between restriction and permissiveness. There is a suggestion of what to do, with room for choice ("into the fields or down the lane"). Mrs. Rabbit had an eye to future independence. We have the unequivocal prohibition, with a cogent reason for it. No room for argument or wheedling there!

Mrs. Rabbit's discipline was effective, as three out of her four children followed her instructions that day. Only Peter went into Mr. McGregor's garden, where, after painful experiences and panic, he barely escaped with his life.

Taking the Consequences

We must give Mrs. Rabbit credit for her handling of Peter when he limped home, later that day, after his horrendous fright in Mr. McGregor's garden, minus his new shoes and his jacket with the brass buttons. Sick at heart and with a bad stomachache, Peter was put to bed by his mother and nursed tenderly with camomile tea. She refrained from lecturing him. Although she did not let him have the blackberries and currant buns that Flopsy, Mopsy, and Cottontail, who had been good little bunnies, had for their supper, she wisely let her son's physical and emotional distress point up the sad consequences of flagrant disobedience.

When the consequences of going against a parent's instructions are not overwhelming or too hazardous, taking these consequences is usually educational. One may need to point out certain connections between cause and effect, but without lecturing or adding insult to injury with an "I told you so."

The statement of a five-year-old, once quoted in *The New Yorker*, "I don't like it here, 'cause everything I do they blame on me," illustrates the viewpoint of the young. The connection between what one does that one has been told not to do and its consequences in the attitudes of others or one's own physical and emotional discomfort is hard to accept.

Adults can point out calmly, and in a manner that is not punishing, the connection between what a youngster has done and the way people respond to his action or the results that have inevitably followed his behavior. That one answers for one's behavior is an idea that takes root gradually through the years. Taking responsibility for one's actions in small ways furthers the development of self-control, too. We need not be discouraged if our children at the age of four or five are full of fanciful alibis to establish their innocence. "I didn't do anything to break that dumb ol' bowl. It just came apart," typifies the logic of a four-year-old who had put the bowl on his head, pretending it was a helmet. "Bowls are to put things in, not to wear as hats.

It's better not to play with things that break easily and weren't meant to be played with," is a statement that may help him view such situations more realistically in the future.

Although the results may not be immediately evident, the effect of living with adults who take the consequences of their behavior is an education in emotional honesty. "I got a ticket for parking too long, and I'll have to pay it. I took a chance when I parked so long in the fifteen-minute zone," tells even a youngster with a hazy idea about parking tickets and parking zones that one acknowledges one's mistakes and pays for them in one way or another.

Consistency and Flexibility

Another component of good discipline is consistency, but consistency needs to be tempered with flexibility or it can become rigidity of a harmful kind.

We might roughly define consistency in discipline as holding certain goals or practices as desirable day after day and certain others as undesirable. Yet certain goals or practices that may be desirable under some conditions would not be under others. This is where flexibility comes in.

Melissa wanted a peanut-butter-and-jelly sandwich half an hour before supper time. Her mother said, "No, but here's a piece of carrot you may have." The next day, arriving home from the afternoon kindergarten session she attended, Melissa asked for a peanut-butter-and-jelly sandwich, and her mother cheerfully made one for her. Melissa's mother, when she could say "Yes," liked to say it wholeheartedly, and that is a part of good discipline, too. No inconsistency was involved, for peanut-butter-and-jelly sandwiches are taboo only immediately before a family meal in Melissa's house, and eating between meals is permissible, depending on what and when you eat.

Destructive Inconsistency

The kind of inconsistency that is confusing and even destructive to a small child is, for instance, being rewarded with laughter and praise for trying to imitate a grown-up dance seen on television one day, and then the next day, when adult company is present, having the same performance greeted with, "Cut it out. I don't want to see you show off that way ever again."

A child could understand being told, "Daddy and I like to see you dance for us, but when we have company of our own, they want to talk to us," but an apparently arbitrary change in his parents' attitude would give him no clues for future behavior.

Unexplained reversal of the permissible and the unacceptable, if it occurs frequently in many different situations, can be damaging. If a mother and father have markedly divergent ideas about what constitutes "good behavior," that, too, can cause difficulties. A study of personality characteristics in nursery school children found that when the parents were usually in agreement in the discipline they believed in, the children were more friendly, spontaneous, and had a firmer sense of belonging in the family. The more widely parents differed in their conceptions and their administration of discipline, the less the children demonstrated those qualities.

In their book *Child Development Research*, Martin and Lois Hoffman say:

Inconsistent discipline apparently contributes to maladjustment, conflict and aggression in the child . . . Studies have repeatedly shown a higher degree of erratic or inconsistent discipline, both within and between parents, to contribute to anti-social behavior. The concept of consistency in discipline is multifaceted and quite poorly understood, although everyone is quite ready to agree that inconsistency is *bad* for children. It is reasonable to assume that consistent behavior by the parent will increase the degree of predictability of the child's environment, and lead to more stable behavior patterns.

If this is the conclusion of the most careful analysis of the research on the subject, parents may justifiably decide that in the "consistency with flexibility" department, you often have to play it by ear!

When Adults Need to Be Firm

When firmness is called for, it is well to keep in mind that one can be immovable and impervious to wheedling and to such accusations as "You are a mean, mean Mommy and I won't love you any more" without becoming harsh or angry. We can be firm, too, without being belittling or tearing down a child's decent opinion of himself. We can make a good, clear "No" stick without adding, "You're always trying to get away with something. You'll end up in trouble when you grow up." Good discipline tells a child, "Even when Daddy and I have to say 'No' to you, we love you and think you are O.K."

The more secure we are in our own strength as parents, and the more we realize how big and powerful we look to the three- through five-year-olds, the more readily we can keep our enforcement of necessary prohibitions good-humored, or at least calm. Anger or threats of punishment are not good teaching tools.

"I'm going over to Tommy's to play," says four-and-a-half-year-old Roy on a Sunday morning.

Roy's parents know that in Tommy's house visitors are not welcome on Sunday in the early hours. Tommy's parents have made it clear to Roy's mother that, much as they like having Roy at other times, the hustle and bustle of getting their five children off to Sunday school after a late breakfast makes one more small boy underfoot just what they do not need.

"Never on Sunday, in the morning, at Tommy's, Roy. You know that. You may go over this afternoon," says Roy's mother. The "not now, but later" substitute is one that small children often accept, but in this instance it proves fruitless.

Roy continues to tease. "Why can't I go? I won't stay much. I'll just be there a tiny second of a minute."

"No, this isn't the time they like company. Sis will read you the comics, if you ask her to." Roy's mother tries, in vain, the time-honored and useful gambit of diverting the boy's attention from what he wants and cannot have to what is permissible.

"Tommy's my friend. He likes me to come over. How do you know they don't want company?"

"Roy, you may *not* go now, and that's that, so you might as well settle down to playing here," his father tells him.

Roy has now worked himself up to such a pitch that he can't stop himself. He makes a rush for the door, and his father catches him. "Roy, you are staying here. We've told you you are not going to Tommy's, and we will not let you go." His father is firm, but still friendly. He keeps to the point at issue and does not say, "Furthermore, sucking your thumb when you don't get what you want is disgraceful in a boy your age."

"If you don't let me go, I'll break everything in this house," declares the boy, standing woefully in the middle of the room and not looking as if he were about to break anything. Silence from his parents.

With one eye on his mother and father, Roy drifts off to his room, where he sulks and sobs for a few minutes. Then he emerges and sheepishly approaches his older sister, who is reading the comics in the Sunday paper. "Wanna read 'em to me?" he asks.

"Don't care if I do," she says nonchalantly.

Parents and Security

A recent study examined the effect on the behavior of preschool children of various parental styles of discipline. The children were divided into three groups.

Group I consisted of boys and girls described as being "self-reliant, self-controlled, interested in exploring their surroundings, and generally contented."

The children in Group II were described as being withdrawn, discontented, and suspicious.

A third group consisted of children who showed

little self-control or self-reliance and who tended to re-treat from unfamiliar experiences.

The parents of the children in the first group were found to be "markedly more consistent, more loving, more secure in the handling of their children, and more likely to accompany a directive with reason." The parents in this group also tended to be more sympathetic and encouraging to their child and to talk more freely to him than did the parents in the other groups. They usually followed through on seeing that the children did as they were told. These mothers and fathers were able to say "No" when that was necessary and to stay with that "No," yet they were not overprotective, nor did they restrict the children unnecessarily.

From these facts, the researchers concluded that firm controls in the preschool years, if parents are warm, are not likely to make children either fearful or over-dependent.

The parents of the children who had poorer self-control tended to be uncertain about their own ability to control their children. Instead of using reason, the mothers of the less self-reliant and confident children were found to be inclined to use ridicule or the "I won't love you any more if you act that way" approach as techniques to control their sons and daughters. Fathers of the less-confident children more often did not follow through on directions they had given.

A Time and Place for Rewards

A disappointed, angry, or frustrated child is en-titled to a substitute activity when he must be denied the one he wants. Giving a substitute is, in such cases, good mental health practice and to be encouraged. We are not "rewarding" the boy or girl who has had a temper tantrum, who has been involved in some mischief, or who has persisted in asking for what he may not have, if, when it is all over, we let him know he is forgiven and back in our good graces. We can afford, both for his well-being and our own, to be affectionate and friendly rather than distant.

When are rewards in order? How do we make the distinction between a reward and a bribe? A reward for achievement or for good behavior under trying circumstances becomes a bribe when a parent puts himself in a bargaining position. Offering some privilege or a tangible advantage to a youngster for giving up what he wants, or would be inclined to do, in favor of what his parents are asking of him may create such a bargaining situation. The difference between offering a substitute activity, a bribe, and a reward is sometimes a matter of phrasing and attitude; but the bribery attitude can color the parent-child relationship if it becomes habitual. A bribe implies buying off a child.

When there is a clear connection between what is offered and what a mother or father is asking the boy or girl to do, bribery is less likely to enter the picture. For example, "If you play by yourself while I finish what I'm doing, I'll get done faster and we can go to the store sooner. Maybe there we can find some of those cookies you like best," is a reasonable handling of a four-year-old's restless demands to know, "When are we going?" To say, "If you play by yourself for fifteen minutes, I'll give you a penny," would put the whole matter on the footing of bribery.

Bribes are usually offered ahead of time, and rewards come after an achievement. If the reward comes as a surprise, so much the better. Indeed, so many of the accomplishments of the preschooler bring him so much satisfaction in themselves that he needs far less of the "carrot in front of the donkey" type of reward that often seems to spur on his older brothers and sisters. A hug and a word of praise may be sufficient for the three- or four-year-old in many situations where a material reward might be of dubious value.

The Delayed Reward

Certainly, for small children rewards should never be offered for anything that involves a long stretch of time, a vague attainment, or more self-control than may be possible. In this class would be "If you are good all week . . ." A week is too long, and besides, what is "good" and who can maintain "goodness" indefinitely? "If you don't wet your bed for a week (or a month) . . ." sets a goal that may be beyond a child's conscious control. "If you don't cry when the doctor gives you a shot . . ." puts a high value on not showing one's feelings and may, as a result, make a youngster anxious.

One trouble with rewards announced in advance, even if they are only in the form of marking achievement with stars pasted on a chart, is that not getting the reward means failure. In our success-oriented society, failure is almost a form of punishment. The atmosphere in which we live inevitably underscores success and failure sufficiently so that parents do not need to go out of their way to emphasize it further.

If one of our long-range goals is that our children become cooperative and learn that achievement for its own sake brings satisfaction, then we will use rewards sparingly with young children. Of course a "celebration," in which the entire family joins when one of its members has made a new step forward, and which comes as a surprise, is always in order. "Incentive rewards" may be useful in a factory, but factory methods are not desirable in the discipline of the young. If we rely on rewards in teaching cooperation, we may find we have developed in our child a sad case of "What is there in it for me?" before he reaches school age.

Punishment: A Last Resort

If rewards are not to play a major role in discipline, what about punishment? If punishment is really necessary, then let it be immediate, swiftly over, and, if possible, related to the behavior it seeks to deter. The old principle that no punishment should last beyond sundown is still valid. Nor should punishment be deferred. "You can't go on the picnic next Saturday" is undesirable, for when Saturday rolls around the child may have forgotten what he did to cause the deprivation, and his parents may even have forgotten that he was to be deprived.

If a five-year-old who has been told repeatedly to bring his bicycle, or wagon, or whatever into the garage or into the entryway continually neglects to do so, depriving him of the use of the bike for the rest of the day is only just. "If you can't remember to take care of it, you aren't big enough to use it this afternoon," is a train of thought a five-year-old can comprehend.

If a three-year-old has been hitting his playmates, brief isolation may be necessary. A small child can understand that "People don't like to be hit. Until you can manage for yourself, you'll have to stay in your room. When you think you are ready to play with them and be friendly, you come and tell me." Here is an opportunity for taking responsibility for one's own behavior, plus the hint that "You can do better."

If punishment should be swift, then spanking would seem to qualify as acceptable, but that it is soon over is about all that can be said in favor of this method of correction. We can assume that some kind of aggressive behavior landed the boy or girl in the situation that led to his being spanked. Physical punishment is demeaning, frustrating, and painful. It stirs up more anger and feelings of hostility and bears no ethically instructive relation to the child's misdeed. It cannot be interpreted by the youngster as "taking the consequences of his wrongdoing." Numerous and extensive studies have shown that physical punishment tends to breed, rather than curtail, aggressiveness. What is more, the parent who spanks gives his child the model of an adult who hits when he is angry, and models are potent teachers.

Spankings tend to reinforce the child's tendency to strike out by way of retaliation. Spankings, from a long-term view, are self-defeating, since they hinder rather advance independence, self-confidence, and self-control. In fact, one study showed that the daughters of mothers who used physical punishment and were severely restrictive tended to be extremely dependent as they were growing up.

When we deprive a child of something as a punishment, we are telling him that we consider it valuable. For many reasons, some families impose fines on even the young children for any infraction of the rules. But to a four- or five-year-old, a fine is apt either to be meaningless or to convey the impression that one can make anything all right by a money payment.

A metropolitan paper recently printed an article by one of its columnists headed, "You Can Go Broke at Our House at the Age of Four." The columnist went on to explain how an elaborate system of fines was used to keep the children's behavior in line. What that writer either did not see, or did not regard as important, was that the four- or five-year-olds in his family were being given a set of values that might haunt the parents later. If we are trying to teach, for example, consideration for the needs and feelings of others, but then allow the payment of a fine to take the place of such consideration, what are we really teaching?

Punishment of any kind, to be effective, needs to be infrequent, or the children become inured to it. If we find it necessary to punish a four- or five-year-old, not just redirect or correct him, several times a day, then it is time to examine the roots of his disobedience.

Chronic Disobedience

Sometimes standards that are so high that a child is always falling short of them may cause him to appear "disobedient" when he is merely acting in a manner quite usual for one at his stage of development. Or, discouraged by his failure to meet his parents' demands and win their approval, he may give up trying and go his own—and decidedly disobedient—way.

Living in crowded quarters with no space in which to be active may make a child so tense and restless that he is constantly getting rid of energy in unacceptable ways.

The child who feels unloved and pushed aside because his parents pay scant attention to him, aside from giving routine care, may be among the conspicuously unruly ones. More time alone with his mother and/or father, just for enjoyment and praise instead of criticism, may bring about a greater degree of cooperativeness on the part of the small child.

Some children are always in trouble because they do not have sufficient legitimate outlets for their energy in play, both alone and with other children. If nobody provides them with or helps them use play materials, and if all the activities they attempt turn out to be in the forbidden category, they despair of finding ways of playing that are satisfactory both to themselves and their parents.

Trying to Communicate

Disobedience, particularly if it occurs over and over again in a particular situation, may be a signal that we are holding a child down to a level of behavior that he has outgrown. Five-and-a-half-year-old Morton was using the only means at his disposal to try to tell his parents that his three-year-old brother's seven o'clock bedtime was too early for him. From the point of view of getting sufficient sleep and of getting the seniority right of staying up later than the younger boy, Morton needed to be allowed at least half an hour more of play or of the company of his parents.

After he had been put to bed, Morton would, night after night, get up and come into the kitchen where his parents were watching TV or chatting. He would find excuses to get up two or three or four times between bedtime and eight o'clock. This disturbed his younger brother, with whom he shared a room, far more than if he had been tucked in bed quietly after the three-year-old was asleep. Usually, he ended up being punished for not staying in bed, as well.

When his parents finally decided that perhaps letting him stay up longer would do away with the nightly impasse and told him they considered him old enough now to have a later bedtime, the jumping out of bed grew less frequent and finally disappeared.

The child who seems to be continually disobeying the rules of the household, like the child who seems unable to understand caution (described in Chapter 8), may be anxious. If his parents are having difficulties in their marriage, are worried about problems with their own aging parents, are under tension in their work lives, or feel discriminated against on account of the racial, ethnic, or religious group to which they belong, their anxiety, though never discussed in the youngster's presence, may create uneasiness in him. Then, not really aware of what he is doing, he is driven to forbidden and irrational behavior. Sometimes he may be helped by a simplified explanation that he can understand about the nature of his parents' troubles, with the assurance that they will find some way out.

Finally, the chronically disobedient preschooler may have some undetected physical disorder that makes him uncomfortable. Discomfort, like anxiety, may impel him to bizarre behavior in the hope that something will relieve the nagging malady.

Balancing Controls

If, as we have stressed before, one of our long-term goals is to have our children during these years begin to take responsibility for their own behavior, we need to look at the effect of various kinds of control. A recent study has shown that when power in the family is exercised entirely by the parents, children tend to feel that responsibility for their behavior rests in some force outside themselves.

In families in which youngsters are rarely restricted, wheedle their parents, and the parents are apathetic or see themselves as helpless or are extremely immature, the youngsters are likely to grow up self-centered and insensitive to the feelings and needs of other people. They are apt to be concerned chiefly with what they themselves need or want.

When parents share the power in the family in appropriate ways by letting children make choices that they are actually capable of making and by helping them understand the reasons for restrictions and rules, boys and girls have a good chance of growing up with the feeling that they are responsible for their own actions. At the same time, the young in such families develop some concern for what other people need.

Respecting the Child

When we look for the causes of behavior, when we adapt the discipline in the family to long-range goals as well as to immediate convenience, we are respecting our children. Part of respecting a child is keeping in mind his needs and his limitations. That also means taking account of his unique personality as well as the phase of development in which he happens to be at the moment.

Of course, as he is becoming domesticated, we expect the youngster to accommodate himself to the rules of the world and the customs of the family, but at times the family can also accommodate itself to its individual members. One way of saying that discipline, ideally, respects each member of the family is to suggest that we try not to treat anyone in the family in such a way as to work a hardship on any other member or on the family as a whole. At the same time, our discipline can be so planned that regulations for the family as a whole do not deprive anyone of what he needs in the way of emotional support, attention or recognition, or consideration for his physical limitations.

Respecting a child also means accepting him as he is and helping him to make the most of his potentialities rather than trying to turn him into the "dream" youngster we may have hoped for. A family can be enriched, both at the moment and on a long-term basis, by differences between its members.

If we can tailor our discipline to respect our children, to regard their desire to grow up as well as their need to be cared for and to be childlike, we can more readily make discipline serve both immediate needs and long-term goals.

5

Questions Need Honest Answers

RUDYARD KIPLING, IN his oft-quoted poem, wrote:

> I keep six honest serving-men
> (They taught me all I knew);
> Their names are What and Why and When
> And How and Where and Who.

The honest serving-men are not unfailingly popular with mothers and fathers; preschoolers seem to work them overtime and sometimes bring up topics difficult for parents to handle. Nevertheless, the young child's questions are his best tools for learning about the world around him, the people in it, and the way they interact with one another.

Questions are usually a sign of a lively curiosity. Such curiosity is basic to learning and to reaching out mentally, emotionally, and socially. Preschool youngsters take little for granted. Naive enough to believe that a simple explanation must exist or that some person is responsible for all events and phenomena, they demand to know, "Who made the sky?" and "Why can't cats talk?" and "What is 'dead'?" as if they were asking nothing more complicated than "What is ice cream made of?" Their faith in their parents' knowledge is boundless, another aspect of their charming naiveté, and impels them to believe we can supply satisfying answers to any inquiry.

Because questioning is so essential to development, it is worth considering the meaning of different varieties of questions to the children, and to us, as well as some effective means of dealing with questions as they come up in daily life.

Questions Serve Numerous Purposes

Not all of a small child's inquiries are by any means merely requests for information. Listening carefully, we will usually be able to detect what lies behind the question as well as the feelings prompting it. How we answer will depend, not on any formula, for none has ever been devised, but on what we sense to be the youngster's need at the moment. We can estimate the amount of understanding he has in the particular field he is asking about and how much he can grasp by way of an answer. The same question at five calls for a fuller explanation than it did at three—and may have a quite different meaning.

Our answer will hinge, too, on our own feelings. At the end of a long day filled with irritations, we might be tempted to meet so innocent an inquiry as "Why does the soap get littler in the water?" with "Can't you see I'm busy? DON'T bother me any more!"

A question may arouse such strong feelings in us that a reply is difficult. "Why doesn't Billy's mother like me?" "Why don't we go to church on Sunday like Grandma does?" "If I'm very, very good, couldn't I have a baby sister for Christmas?" or some other query that hits us in a sensitive spot may tempt us to cut off the questioner.

The way his mother or father receives an inquiry may teach a youngster much more than any facts offered in reply. If he or she discovers that asking is acceptable, the way is kept open for the satisfying of curiosity in other areas, another day.

Conversation Starters

Preschoolers often use a question when they want to start a conversation, as Keith did. This three-year-old came out of the house, observed his father absorbed in changing the spark plugs on his automobile, and said, "Whatcha doing that for?"

"So the car will run better," his father told him. Although Keith may not have been aware of it, the question behind his spoken one was, "Are you too busy to talk with me? Is that car more important to you than I am?"

His father's prompt, willing, and factual response told him something about his father as well as why men tinker with cars. Keith's feeling that his father would not be angry or tell him to go away if he talked to him, even when he was busy, was reinforced. The man-to-man, comprehensible reply also conveyed the impression to the little boy, "You are worthy of a sensible answer."

Had his father made a habit of saying something like, "I'm putting the thingummies on the whosis," which even a three-year-old could recognize as being talked down to, Keith's self-esteem might have been lowered a notch or two. A teasing reply, such as, "There's a troll living under the hood and I'm taking his tonsils out because he had a sore throat," might, for some children, under some circumstances, give the feeling, "You and I know when a joke is a joke." However, Keith's father felt intuitively that a fanciful answer was not what his son was looking for at that moment.

As conversation openers, or for that matter, as attention getters, questions surely have a legitimate place. Consider how much more socially sophisticated was Keith's "Whatcha doing that for?" than his behavior might have been only a few short months ago. Then, he might have stood behind his father and given him a playful swat or called loudly "Boo!" The question demonstrated Keith's interest in somebody else's activity and a desire to interact with him.

When a Question Is Not THE Question

When Melinda Ryan, four and a half years old, pestered her mother with a torrent of empty questions, one following another without waiting for a reply— "What's this?" "What's it for? "Where did you get it?" "How does it work?" "Can I work it?"—her mother knew that not just Melinda's inquiring mind, but restlessness and boredom were at the root of these inquiries. An interesting occupation, not reproof for the stream of questions nor answers to them, was Melinda's need.

Mrs. Ryan would say, "Melinda, how about getting out some colored paper and your scissors? I'll fix you some paste and you make me a cutout picture I can put up here in the kitchen. Make one to surprise Daddy when he comes home, too." This and similar pursuits that Mrs. Ryan reserved for just such times tended to alter what the mother called Melinda's "pestiferous moods."

Various kinds of unmet needs may contribute to a youngster's being restless and bored. Insufficient companionship with those his own age is a possible cause. How to provide that is discussed in Chapter 3. He may need more opportunities to practice independence, the topic of Chapter 9. More opportunities for vigorous or noisy play may answer the need of other youngsters; this topic is taken up in Chapter 10.

Sometimes questions stem from a basic, indefinable uneasiness. These cannot be dismissed as "just to get attention." Substitute "reassurance" for "attention" in that statement, and you may have a more accurate diagnosis. A youngster may, for some reason, feel pushed aside. Perhaps a new baby or a visitor in the family seems to him to have displaced him in his parents' affections. Perhaps he has been scolded too frequently for misbehaving. Possibly a parent, under pressure and harried, has not been able to pay as much attention to him as usual. His questions, often utterly inane, are a plea for recognition.

Wanting reassurance when one is troubled is hardly an offense. If the disheartened boy or girl pelts us with a barrage of "Why do I have to play outside?

Why do I have to wear a jacket? Why can't I go across the street? Why do you have to go to the store?" and so on, we can try an extra bit of affectionate attention. It may be more effective than either reasonable answers or attempts to stem the tide of "Why's?" Such affection would not be "rewarding" the nagging, whining questions; it would merely be having the good sense to see beneath them to the real difficulty.

Questions About Family Crises

When parents are disturbed about such troubles as an impending move to another city, a sharp decline in the family's finances, the loss of a father's or a mother's job, the threat of a serious illness, physical or mental, to some member of the family, even young children seem to sense it. At such times we may get a barrage of questions from our preschooler about everything except the one question to which he wants an answer. He wants to know what is wrong and why we are worried, but he cannot, or dare not, put that into words.

Young children deserve a simple explanation. If they do not feel shut out, and if their parents are not overwhelmed by the event, the children often show relief and surprising stamina. The assurance that "Daddy and Mommy will take care of you, no matter what happens," and that "We know what to do," can relieve them greatly and perhaps make it possible for their real and justified fears to come out in questions.

Discussing family crises with children is the subject of *What To Tell Your Child About Birth, Death, Divorce and Other Family Crises*, by Helen S. Arnstein.

This book deals with explaining these circumstances in more detail than is possible here, and it can be extremely helpful.

The Stalling Device

Questions play a major part in the gentle art of stalling at which many preschoolers are adept. Although five-year-olds tend to be less prone to this delaying tactic at bedtime than threes or fours, they often return to it as the best method of postponing separation from their parents' company. Ned was a quite competent five-year-old, but when his father or mother would tuck him in for the night, he could come up with queries that would keep one of his parents talking to him for ten minutes to half an hour, or more.

Ned did have lively and wide-ranging interests. To give him his due, he undoubtedly was eager to know the answers when he inquired, "Are fishes unhappy sometimes?" "What is an earthquake?" "Who makes them?" "What if all the daddies didn't go to work ever again?" "What's being rich?" "Do we know anybody who is rich?" "Are rich people bad?"

Ned's astuteness was proved not only by the originality of what he sought to know, but also by his canny observation of the subjects that would keep his father or mother talking. Praiseworthy as were their efforts to give their son explanations in language he could understand, they were allowing themselves to be exploited. They might have done better to say, "That's something to talk about tomorrow, Ned. It's too long a story for tonight." Then, if they remembered to bring up the subject the next day, the boy would not have felt his

questions were unwelcome, though in broad daylight he might have been less interested in what his parents had to say on these abstract and knotty points.

Sometimes a youngster will ask a question when the adult is obviously busy with other matters or is hurrying him to do something he is not pleased about having to do.

"Why do you always pick the worst time to ask the biggest question?" his mother said in despair one day. The boy's nine-year-old sister happened to be in the room, and, as older sisters will, she answered for him. "He knows you won't have time for a long, long story, and he just doesn't want to hear too much," she told their mother. Since both the boy's parents enjoyed talking at length, the girl was probably onto part of the truth.

Information-seeking Questions

Compared to questions that have their origin chiefly in a need to relieve feelings, inquiries prompted by genuine intellectual curiosity seem relatively simple to handle. No matter how well informed we may be, we cannot hope to have a ready explanation for all that a preschooler from time to time wants to know about. Nor can we breathe a sigh of relief and think, "At least we've disposed of *that*," when we have answered a question once. The same request for information will probably crop up again, perhaps phrased differently, and require a fuller explanation next time.

Parents are not diminishing their son's or daughter's faith in them if they say, "I don't know, but let's find out together." Libraries and librarians, especially in the children's section, are in the business of helping people find answers by directing them to materials that can be useful. Three or four is not too early an age for being taken to the neighborhood public library and discovering that books, even though one cannot read them oneself, often hold interesting answers. Many libraries also have pictures, films, and other visual aids to information.

Often, we may not find answers designed for the three- or four-year-old. We will need to interpret material intended for an older child and translate it into words and concepts our preschooler can understand. Too much information can turn off a preschooler's interest. The important point is to let him see that finding answers is possible and pleasant, and that we are willing to cooperate in doing so.

Clearing Up Confusion

Small children have frequently been mulling over a subject before they put their interest into a spoken question. They may have evolved an explanation of their own that is far removed from the facts. Their notion of how airplanes fly, or what elephants like to eat, or how the world began, or such ideas, may be utterly confused. We may get an inkling of misconceptions that had best be cleared up if we turn the question back, with "You tell me what you think." The reply may also give us a clue as to what the youngster really wants to know. We may have trouble not laughing out loud when we hear what the three- or four-year-old has to say, but since being made to feel foolish is a question-stopper, let us refrain from showing our amusement.

Questions seeking information not only deserve honest answers but deserve to be treated with respect. If a four-year-old's notion of why the moon is in the sky during the day or what makes the sun come up in the morning is so charmingly whimsical that we cannot resist telling it to all our friends, at least we should know better than to relate it in his presence.

Jerome Bruner, a respected psychologist and educator, in *On Knowing, Essays for the Left Hand*, says this about how children learn:

The opposite of understanding is not merely ignorance or "not knowing." To understand something is, first, to give up some other way of conceiving of it. . . . The development of the general idea comes from the first round of experience with concrete embodiments of ideas that are close to a child's life.

If our answers to his questions are to expand a small child's real understanding, then those explanations need to be in terms that are familiar to him. "Did the first people in the world live in very old houses like Mrs. Page lives in?" asks a four-year-old to whom the rambling, turn-of-the-century frame house of an elderly neighbor seems absolutely ancient. The answer to that inquiry may lead us to tell about how people lived in caves. If he has never seen a cave, and it is more than likely that he has not, we may say, "A cave is a big hole in the side of a hill. Some caves are quite small, so small that it would be hard to sit down in them. The caves that people lived in were usually big enough so that a man as big as Daddy could stand up in them, although the cave people weren't as tall as Daddy. There might be room in a cave for five or six or even more people to lie down and sleep. Of course they didn't have beds to sleep on, or tables or chairs. There are no windows in caves, either, and it was often cold and wet and, we would think, terribly uncomfortable, and full of bugs, and of smoke from the fire they built inside the cave."

Such homely details out of his own experience give a youngster facts he can understand, yet do not picture primitive life as a perpetual "cook-out" with contemporary zippered, waterproof equipment.

"Any subject can be taught to anybody at any age in some form that is honest," Bruner says, but he cautions against the pitfall of oversimplifying and pretti-

fying a complicated subject to the point that it becomes
not at all an honest portrayal.

Questions About Conduct

This caution about explanations is especially ap-
plicable to those most difficult questions that touch on
justice and law, war and peace, life and death, and similar topics on which neat, clear-cut explanations cannot
be furnished.

If a five-year-old has heard, as Sylvie had, that some
children do not have enough to eat or a place to live,
the child may demand, "Why don't they just make
everybody in the whole world share everything and
then everyone would have enough? Can't the supermarket man give all the hungry people all that peanut
butter and jelly and oranges he has in the store?"

Sylvie's father, when his miniature political econ-
omist posed this question to him, told her that "sharing" was difficult enough when it involved only Sylvie
and her sisters sharing their collected candy on Trick-or-
Treat night. Even then, he reminded her, there had
been arguments and tears because nobody was satisfied
that the division was "fair."

How could you divide things up "fairly" among all
the millions of people in the world who need and
who want different things? Who would decide what
was "enough" or "right" for each one? Maybe
when you grow up, Sylvie, you'll help people who
are hungry or who haven't a place that's nice to live
in. There are lots of ways you can be a helper to
other people.

Inadequate as he knew his explanation was, Sylvie's father felt he had at least let her know that it was all right for little girls to think about such questions. He had not painted either an entirely dark or an entirely rosy picture, but he had tried to show her that solutions to some human problems are hard to find.

We can take care in discussing human relations not to encourage a sharp separation between the "good guys" and the "bad guys," or to give the impression that if a person has one quality we do not like, we then want nothing to do with him. Three- and four-year-olds who are coming to terms with their own consciences tend to see right and wrong as at opposite poles, with no blending at the edges. (This is discussed further in Chapter 7.)

That we like different people for different qualities they may possess needs to be emphasized over and over. Young children tend to be rigid in their thinking and harsh in their judgments, because their own controls are still not in the best working order.

"Don't you like Aunt Fran any more? You told Daddy she talked too much," demands four-year-old Freddy, who finds his great-aunt Fran fun. "Won't she come here again? I like her a lot."

Freddy's mother resisted the temptation to lecture about eavesdropping and explained that she, too, loved Aunt Fran, but that everybody has some faults and sometimes we may get a little angry at someone, although we still like them and we get over being angry.

"You mean like when you tell me you love me even when I do something bad?" Freddy asked, taking a giant stride in understanding personal relationships.

When to Tell the Truth About Myths

Young children's questions may also be hard to deal with because they hit at one or another of the myths we enjoy. We do not want to destroy children's pleasure in Santa Claus or any other favorite myth, yet we are safest if we do not put ourselves in a position that allows them to accuse us of deliberately fooling them. If we avoid telling a child anything that we will later have to "untell" him, we are in a better position to retain his confidence and to spare him the confusion of disillusionment. We can be truthful without being cynical or spoiling the pleasure of pretending, but at the same time we can be clear about what is a fact and what is pretense. The children may elect to cling to the myth, but at least they know *we* know the difference.

The Easter Rabbit is such a myth. We may, quite justifiably and unconsciously, enjoy the illusion ourselves. Surely it is entertaining to watch the children's delight in a basket of prettily colored eggs the Easter Rabbit has presumably left at the door. Without acknowledging it, perhaps we would sometimes like to believe in a bit of magic ourselves.

In one family, the four-and-a-half-year-old was perplexed and resentful. She had heard rumors from a playmate that "The Easter Bunny is just for babies and is a lie." Still, in nursery school the talk had been about the coming arrival of Easter baskets purveyed by the miraculous rabbit. These stories had the support of the teacher herself. The mother in this family, annoyed at both her child's playmates and the teacher, was at a loss in trying to resolve her daughter's demand to know whether the Easter Rabbit was "true." She waited for her husband to come home and help her pick up the pieces, emotionally and intellectually, for the girl.

This youngster had a favorite stuffed dog with whom she carried on long conversations. "Doggie" was a comfort to her when she was lonely or discouraged. Doggie had a personality of his own, and the little girl frequently reported what Doggie liked and did not like and what he had been doing while she was out. Doggie was playing a useful part in her growing up, and at this point he came in handily to assist the father in giving an honest answer to the searching question, "Is the Easter Bunny true?"

"The Easter Bunny," he told his daughter, "is something like your friend Doggie. You know a real, live dog couldn't talk or play the way Doggie does, but you like to pretend he can, don't you?

"When you are tired or have to play by yourself, Doggie is good company, isn't he? He makes you feel good, even though you know he isn't a real dog like Spot over at your cousin's house."

The little girl nodded solemnly, apparently quite able to go along with such reasoning. "Doggie loves me and I love him," she declared.

Her father took a deep breath and hoped she would be able to follow the jump from Doggie's being pretend to the Easter Bunny's being pretend. "Pretending about Easter Bunnies is fun, just the way talking to Doggie is fun for you. Lots of stories we like are pretend. As long as you know they are pretend, it's O.K. We don't have to spoil anybody's fun who likes to pretend."

His daughter looked a bit sad. "Will I still get a

basket from the Easter Bunny?" she asked plaintively. Alas, the belief in myths often has a materialistic basis!

"Of course, there'll be an Easter basket for you on the breakfast table on Sunday, and then Mommy and I'll hide the eggs in it for you and you can hunt for them. It will be a nice pretending, won't it?" The girl agreed it would be. She snuggled up on her father's lap, satisfied that he was not fooling her, and pleased, though she could not have told why, that she was allowed to keep her cherished imaginary creatures.

A youngster who has bridged the gap between fact and fancy in one context can usually do so more readily in a comparable situation, without feeling cheated or losing his trust in his parents' veracity.

"Where Do Babies Come From?"

Answering the questions we hope the children will ask during their preschool years about the difference between the sexes and where babies come from is not far removed from answering the other types of questions seeking information that we have been discussing. Our answers give our sons and daughters sex information, but that is only one facet of the broader experience described as "sex education." The following chapter is concerned with that far larger aspect of a child's development.

Our feelings about questions touching on sex are likely to be different from our attitude toward other questions. Even in these days of outspokenness about sexual relations on the screen, in print, and in the conversation of many adults, it is still the most intimate of topics. Sex may be surrounded by feelings left over from our own childhood. Few grown persons can honestly say that they can answer their children's questions on this aspect of human relations as matter-of-factly as they can answer those about, say, electricity or why leaves are green, no matter how casually they may talk about sex with their contemporaries.

The story is told of a small girl who asked her mother how babies "get borned." Her mother said, "Come and sit down here next to me and I'll tell you." She gave her daughter an explanation and then asked her if she wanted to know anything else.

"Uh huh. I want to know why I had to come and sit next to you for you to tell me all that." This illustrates how special the imparting of sex information is even to those of us who feel able to dispense facts clearly.

Yet, many of the principles that prevail in answering other kinds of questions hold true in this field. The same question, for example, "Where was I before I was born?" calls for a somewhat fuller answer when a five-year-old propounds it than might have been appropriate when that child was two years younger. Children tend to forget the answers to their questions about reproduction just as they do explanations of other phenomena. They may also ask the same question a week, a month, or a year later just to be sure that asking is acceptable or to discover whether our reply will contain the same information. We should not be discouraged if, in spite of the most careful explanation, our son or daughter clings to his own ideas and rejects the more accurate ones we have tried to instill. Learning takes time, especially when the material to be assimilated

138

may be less clear or palatable than his fantasies.

Understand the Question

Just as in answering other kinds of questions, before giving a reply we must be sure we are clear as to what it is the youngster wants to know. An oft-repeated and probably fictitious anecdote tells of a parent who gave his child a complete story of the reproductive process in response to the question "Where did I come from?" only to be told, "That's O.K., but there's a new boy in kindergarten and he comes from New York, and I wanted to know where I come from." That story has a moral for all of us. We need not give a child more information than he is asking for, as too much can turn him off as readily as does too little.

We can be more helpful if we first determine what notions he already has. We may be amazed at the distorted explanation he has concocted out of his imagination and half-understood remarks made by us and others.

Questions about anatomical differences and reproduction are part of a youngster's healthy curiosity. We want to let him feel that asking these questions is acceptable and that we are ready to answer, or, if we cannot answer right at that moment, we will talk over his questions just as soon as we can. Initiating such discussion then becomes our responsibility. Children frequently ask their questions relating to sex, just as they ask other complicated ones, at inopportune moments, because they sense that we are preoccupied and will need to make our answer brief. A long explanation may be more than they are seeking.

A parent does well to leave the way open for more questions as a youngster is ready to ask them. Our willingness to answer, whether we are fluent with all the facts or hesitant, is the foundation of sound sex education.

As for what to say to those most frequent of the preschoolers' questions, about where babies come from and how boys and girls differ, the precise words and phrases have to be our own. If we feel, in looking back at what we said afterward, that we did not include a fact that might have been called for, we must remember that we will have other chances. Dr. Fritz Redl, who has been an authority on discussing children's sex perplexities for many years, has said that if he felt he had made no more than twenty-five mistakes in talking to a boy for half an hour, he congratulated himself.

For the child under six, the occasion for asking questions concerning where babies are before they are born and how they "get born" is usually either his own mother's pregnancy or that of a relative or a neighbor.

Using Correct Terms

Some children's erroneous ideas about birth involve mothers becoming pregnant by eating something. The same idea occurred to some primitive tribes. If we talk about the baby being "in its Mommy's tummy," we reinforce that misconception. It is better to emphasize that a baby grows in a "special place" inside its mother. That place is called the uterus or the womb. Never mind if the listener pays scant attention to that term. Giving the special place a name makes it clearer that the baby is not mixed up with the food his mother eats. We can go on to say that the baby is warm and comfortable and safe in that special place until it is big enough to be born.

Then will probably come the question, "How does it get out?" Children, aware of the openings through which they have bowel movements and through which they urinate, may conclude that babies exit through one of these apertures. Again, we can explain that mothers have a special place, called the vagina, that stretches to be big enough to let the baby out when the time comes.

We may get the question, "Does that hurt?" A "natural childbirth" mother's answer will be special. But whatever her experiences during delivery, she can afford to say something to the effect that it may hurt, and mothers go to the hospital to have babies so the doctors and nurses can help the baby come out. We can go easy on the pains of childbirth and talk about the fact that "Mommies are so glad to have the baby that they forget if it hurts a little."

If a child asks to see the place the baby comes out, we can tell him it is between a mother's thighs and draw a simple diagram to illustrate. Using one's own body to demonstrate is not recommended, as this is likely to be more sexually stimulating than factually informative.

Little girls may be delighted to know that they can be mothers when they grow up, but for little boys the news that only girls grow up to be mommies can be discouraging. They are usually reassured if they are told that it takes both a mother and a father to have a baby, and that boys grow up to be daddies.

Usually, the "What do daddies do to make a baby?" or "How does the baby get started?" type of question is not asked immediately. A youngster has enough to think over in knowing that a baby grows inside its mother.

Just Give the Facts

The question about how a baby gets started, from a four- or five-year-old, is not a request for a description of sexual intercourse but for biological facts. "A baby is started when a tiny cell from the father's body joins a tiny cell in the mother's body. Cells are too small to see, but the baby grows from these cells coming together," is a better explanation than talking about a father's "planting a seed in the mother." The "planting" notion may add to any confusions a small child already has. Discussing fertilization in flowers, fish, or other animals has proved to be far from helpful in straightening out a youngster's perplexities.

More details about how the union of cells occurs are infrequently asked for until after the age of six. But we may as well be prepared to repeat the other explanations we have already made. Many children are not sure they want to believe that babies grow inside their mothers. They may cling to their fantasies.

One mother was shocked to hear her four-year-old tell a neighbor that her baby sister had been bought at the store. "You remember, I told you that a baby is inside its mother before it is born," she said to her daughter. "Yes, I know you told me that, but I was afraid Mrs. Peters would laugh at me if I said that," was the answer.

Just what combination of feelings produced this state of mind would be impossible to say. Perhaps it was the youngster's own disbelief, or distaste for the idea, or an intuitive doubt about the propriety of talking about so delicate a subject, or more likely a combination of all those. Each child interprets and assimilates information in his own way, whether it be about reproduction or any other subject.

Different but Equal

The difference between boys and girls is another concern of preschoolers and is almost sure to precipitate questions. If a child has no siblings, he or she has probably been, or may profitably be, provided with opportunities of seeing both boys and girls of his or her own age without clothes on. Seeing children of the same sex nude is as informative as seeing those of the opposite sex, since one of a child's unspoken questions may be, "Am I all right the way I am?" Observing that there are others who are essentially the same is reassuring. It takes the three- or four-year-old a while to absorb the fact that there are two, and only two, sexes. For all he knows there might be half a dozen!

In answering a little girl's question, "What's he got there hanging down?" when she first takes notice of the boy's penis, a mother can tell her that boys have a penis just as their fathers do. Girls have a vagina and womb like their mother's. If you are born a boy you always stay a boy and grow up to be a man, "like Daddy." If you are born a girl, you always stay a girl and grow up to be a woman, with breasts, "like Mommy." She may want to add that since boys urinate (or make wee-wee, or whatever household term is used) through their penis, it is easier for them to stand up when doing so, whereas girls are more comfortable sitting down.

Being absolutely definite about boys remaining boys and girls remaining girls, and about the desirableness of belonging to either sex helps clear up any worries about losing or having lost that dramatic male organ. We can also take care to phrase our answers to questions about the difference between boys and girls so that boys do not seem to be "the haves" and girls "the have-nots."

The question of why observing other children their own age undressed sets doubts at rest but observing adult nudity may arouse anxiety in some children is discussed in Chapter 6.

When a Child Asks No Questions

That a youngster nearing six has never asked any questions about reproduction or differences between the sexes does not necessarily mean he is disinterested or unconcerned. Since these years are the time when confusions are quite readily cleared up, we may want to make it easy for our son or daughter to bring up the subject. The arrival of a baby either in his own home or in the home of a relative or a friend is often a convenient occasion for bringing up the subject with the child who has asked no questions. If a parent can arrange to take the nonquestioner to see the baby, and it is of the opposite sex, she might casually point out the difference. If the youngster sees the mother nursing the baby, that may be an introduction to the topic of "where babies come from."

If we do not have access to a new baby, we may help a youngster ask a question that is on his mind by saying something like, "When I was little I used to think that babies were ordered from a store. Where did you think they came from when you were little?" Knowing that a parent was once in doubt or had made wrong conjectures may help a child express his confusion.

Another approach to the nonquestioner is to read him one of the excellent books for young children about babies. *The Wonderful Story of How You Were Born*, by Sidonie M. Gruenberg, or *I'm Going To Have a Baby*, by Laura Z. Hobson, are among the good ones for four-and-a-half- and five-year-olds.

Learning from Questioning

The ever-amazing flow of questions in all fields often reveals what is on a youngster's mind, but it can also wear down parental patience. If we are aware of what different types of questions may be telling us, as explained here, and if we recognize how questioning contributes to mental and social development, our tolerance for a child's curiosity may expand. Responding appropriately and not shutting off queries may make the difference between a child's keeping and cultivating the spirit of inquiry and the desire to know, and his becoming indifferent or resistant to learning now and when he goes to school. Giving him the conviction that "It is all right to ask" is a sound foundation for his learning throughout life, for good questioners tend to make good learners.

6

Masculinity
. . . Femininity

I N ORDER TO grow into a reasonably healthy, happy
personality, a small person needs to feel he is "all
right" and likable. Basic to that self-esteem is the conviction that it is good to be a boy or to be a girl. A child
needs to feel that both sexes are loved and valued. Out
of such attitudes come the boy's desire to grow into
a man and take on the "manly" characteristics our culture demands, and the girl's wish to become appropriately feminine.

The cultivation of masculinity and femininity is
neither direct nor entirely obvious. We shall consider
what we mean by these terms, and how parents can
create an atmosphere that fosters the qualities involved.
Related to this is a preschooler's attitude toward his
own body. How do we further healthy attitudes in this
area?

Expectations and Behavior

Each society, anthropologists tell us, prescribes certain propensities and activities for its men and for its women. In raising children, parents around the world try to instill the behavior that conforms to the standard of masculinity and femininity in their culture or their own segment of that society. Martin and Lois Hoffman, in *Review of Child Development Research,* describe the standards a society sets for manliness and womanliness as two separate clusters of wishes, feelings, and external attributes—one cluster for the males and another for the females. Once such a cluster has been acquired by an individual, it acts as an internal judge or monitor, approving or disapproving of his or her sentiments or actions. That cluster becomes a part of conscience, as will be discussed in Chapter 7.

By the age of six, and in some respects far earlier, a youngster usually has a fairly good grasp of those qualities associated with "What mommies do" and "What daddies do" in many aspects of daily living, although all their concepts may not be entirely clear.

What Makes the Difference?

Is behavior we call masculine or feminine rooted in the biological makeup of each sex, or does it stem from external pressures? Some students of human behavior attribute the differences in the aptitudes of each sex to the action of hormones, although that hormonal difference is generally agreed not to be present in children of preschool age. Other authorities assert that sex roles are acquired in early childhood. A boy or girl learns to act in ways his or her family considers appropriate for each sex. He (or she) comes to believe that he (or she) possesses some of the characteristics of the parent of the same sex and identifies with that parent. A boy or girl models himself, often without realizing it, on the example set by that parent.

In identifying with a model, a youngster behaves as if events happening to that model were also happening to him. Four-year-old Lola had often heard that she looked like her pretty mother. When her mother dressed up to go out, the small girl took on her mother's pleasure in looking well groomed and attractive. Like most young children, Lola believed that inner resemblance accompanied outward similarity, although she could not have put that belief into words. If she looked like her mother, then she must be like her mother, Lola reasoned.

Another source of learning the behavior typical of one's sex is the tendency of human beings to take on the behavior they perceive as being expected of them. This is part of that "self-fulfilling prophecy" explained in Chapter 1. One becomes, to a great extent, what one is repeatedly told one will become.

A third road that leads to masculine and feminine characteristics is that children discover that they will win acceptance and approval more readily when they conform to the standards held for members of their own sex. A four-year-old boy in a nursery school was part of a group playing they were spacemen. "Now I'm going to be a spaceman painting a picture," he declared, stopping in his play in front of the easels set up in a corner of the room.

"Spacemen don't paint pictures, you dope!" his companions jeered at him, although in this school both boys and girls enjoyed painting and it was not held to be the prerogative of one sex. At the same time, a girl who wanted to be a "spacelady" was rudely told, "Girls aren't in space capsules. You get away from us."

Stereotypes Get in Our Way

In a magazine article, Florence Howe stated:

Though there is no evidence that their early physical needs are different from or less than boys', girls are offered fewer activities even in kindergarten. They may sit and watch while boys, at the request of the female teacher, change the seating arrangement in the room. Of course, it's not simply a matter of physical exercise or ability: Boys are learning how to behave as men, and girls to be "ladies" who enjoy "being waited on."

This quotation is not from a periodical published in 1910, 1930, or even 1950. It is cited as evidence that "Sexual Stereotypes Start Early," the title of the article, which appeared in the *Saturday Review* of October 16, 1971. The article is an adaptation of an address Professor Howe gave, at the invitation of Columbia's Women's Liberation, to the Superintendents' Work Conference. The author contends that our schools, in spite of a preponderance of women teachers, prepare girls to be second-class citizens, always "assisting," but rarely leading.

Labeling some attitudes and behavior as masculine and others as feminine has unfortunate consequences, since it leads us, and the children, to think in stereotypes. The small girl who is not sure whether she wants a chocolate or a vanilla ice-cream bar and wavers in making her choice, may hear from her father, "Just like a woman to keep changing her mind. None of them know what they want." Again, she may hear, over and over, that certain tasks are "women's work," and that "men are better at using tools," or keeping account of money, or thinking straight. Small boys, if they cry over a minor bump, or betray their disappointment, or have their feelings hurt easily, are likely to be told, "Men don't act that way. Boys have to be able to take it."

Forcing Responsibility

One father, in saying good-bye to his three-year-old son each morning, would say, in a joking manner, "Now you be the man in the family and look after your mother and your sisters today." To the boy, this was no joke, and manliness seemed to be a burden. He knew he needed his mother to take care of him. The insistence on the stereotype became a threat of responsibility he found overwhelming. More than the Women's Liberation movement has made it necessary for us to reexamine some of our cherished myths about "the right behavior" for each sex.

Research on the behavior of preschoolers has demonstrated that belligerence, perhaps because the stereotype has become familiar to them, is more frequent among small males than among females. One way the three- to five-year-old boys exhibit that aggressiveness is in their play with dolls, which take far more of a beating from the boys who play with them than from the girls. Even when little girls are pretending that the dolls have been "very bad," they do not get as violent in pretending to punish them as do the boys. Perhaps a healthy move away from the myths about appropriate sex behavior is the fact that in most nursery schools the boys are allowed to play, in their own way, with dolls. According to a study in one kindergarten, the more masculine boys, when playing with the dolls, showed that they perceived the feminine role both as a caretaking and a powerful one.

How Children See Their Parents

Results of tests to determine how small children view each parent reveal that father is seen as "more aggressive, punitive, and even dangerous than mother." In many households, father is also perceived as the one who is more skilled in using his hands, repairing household appliances, and the one who is looked to for decisions regarding expenditures.

Bearing out the results of such research, while four-year-old Noah was visiting his grandmother one day, she attempted, none too skillfully, to replace a broken plug at the end of a lamp cord. Noah observed her efforts for a minute or two, and then advised her, "You better wait 'till Grandpa gets home and he'll fix it. My Daddy is the fixer at my house. He says ladies aren't good at that."

Since his grandmother knew that Noah's grandfather did not conform to the image of being "a good fixer," she determined to make short work both of the repair job and of Noah's stereotype. "Girls and women can fix things just as well as men can, Noah. And you know what? Some men don't like being 'fixers' even though they like being men, and your grandpa is like that."

Whether or not the introduction of this point of view widened Noah's conception of what is proper for men and women, his faith in his father's competence is a far healthier attitude than the one seen too often in films, TV comedies, and comic strips. The mass media, in portraying men as blustering, but bungling, and women as achieving their goals through manipulation, indirection, and, too often, duplicity, are not giving the young a picture of either sex calculated to build mutual respect or trust, even when the satire is amusing to adults.

Children tend to "catch" their parents' feelings about the sex each belongs to as well as about the opposite sex. An unhappily married woman, or one who has no husband, may voice the opinion, all too frequently, that men are not to be relied on. She may, too, show by her actions that she considers them untrustworthy. Such an attitude tends to rub off on her daughters and to make her sons feel that manliness is not safe.

A mother who is angry because she is a woman, or who looks down on all activities labeled as feminine, may prejudice her children against the rightness of being female. Comparable attitudes on the part of a father have, of course, a similar detrimental effect.

Are We Unfair to Our Girls?
Alice Rossi, a sociologist concerned with the position of women and a reasonably moderate leader of Women's Lib, has long maintained that in raising girls to conform to the picture of a docile, helpful,

somewhat dependent, caretaking person, we are supplying society with the stuff of which are made good assistants to men in laboratories, factories, offices, or health and educational institutions. We are not, even today, raising our girls to become leaders in their own right in many occupations. Our girls tend to grow up believing they are less important, less competent, less courageous than boys are.

So far, young children whose mothers have paid jobs and whose parents share household and child-caring responsibilities still seem to absorb from the general atmosphere the older idea of "men's work" and "women's work," even though the pattern in their own home does not tally with it. With the increasing number of families in which the wife's continuing education and/or her satisfaction and success in her work influence the plans of the entire family as much as does the husband's need for training, a good job, and gratifying leisure pursuits, we might speculate whether the trend will give small boys and girls a more up-to-date impression of the expanding boundaries of masculine and feminine behavior.

Do Boys Pay a Price for Privilege?

Research as well as observation confirms the belief that greater freedom, power, and value are still attached to the part the man plays in our society. Yet life is not entirely full of extra privileges for males. In the great majority of homes, however enlightened they may be, boys are taught, from the time they sally forth to join the other children in the neighborhood on the sidewalk, to keep their affectionate, gentler tendencies

bottled up. Demonstrating such sentiments is considered more appropriate for girls.

Boys are expected to prepare themselves to be less dependent on the attitudes and opinions of others, studies have concluded. If a small boy is shut out by his playmates and is, as a result, uneasy and apprehensive, he tends to get less sympathy at home than a girl would under similar circumstances.

A small boy who busies himself with building blocks or construction toys, in preference to playing with other children, may be approved for his self-reliance. His sisters are expected to be friendly and make themselves agreeable to others to a greater extent than he.

How Does Sexual Identity Develop?

Everyone, consciously or unconsciously, has some idea's about himself as a member of his own sex. Everyone regards himself, or herself, as having some traits that are owing to or a part of sex membership. The degree to which an individual thinks of himself or herself as masculine or feminine is described by Martin and Lois Hoffman in A *Review of Child Development Research* as his or her sexual identity. This attitude toward himself is only one of a set of interlocking beliefs, which, taken together, make up a child's total self-concept.

Just how sexual identity is established, psychologists and members of other disciplines concerned with human behavior are not in agreement, but in general one's picture of oneself as masculine or feminine comes from several sources.

First is an awareness of being like the parent of one's own sex and different from the parent of the opposite sex. Then, too, a youngster gets a sense of sex identity from the degree to which he or she is interested in and able to master the skills, scaled down to size, appropriate for that sex.

As an illustration, look at Mrs. Chase's experience with her three-and-a-half-year-old daughter, Elaine, who wanted to "help" bake a cake. Mrs. Chase baked in the old-fashioned manner, without a mix. All the dry ingredients had to be carefully sifted and measured. She had been through the assistance to be had from the young with Elaine's two elder brothers, both of whom would invariably lose interest after a minute or two of sifting sugar or flour. Not so Elaine. Mrs. Chase remembers:

It was uncanny. Elaine stuck with the flour, sifting even though her little hands must have gotten tired. She was entirely different from what the boys had been like. She stayed with it, right next to me, doing what I told her to until the batter went into the pans and we put some in a little pan for a cake of her own. Baking was her bag, and no mistake. Then she said in a sort of prissy tone I'd never heard before, "Now I'm just like Mommy. I'm a good baker."

Not all girls are more domestic than their brothers at an early age, but those who do derive satisfaction from pursuits traditionally regarded as feminine have their sense of sex identity reinforced.

Elaine's greater persistence in staying with the baking probably stemmed in part from a feeling that she was expected to enjoy it. That enjoyment, in turn, was enhanced as Mrs. Chase took trouble to find spots in which Elaine could participate. She identified with the girl's interest in helping. Identification is a two-way street. A youngster's sense of sex membership deepens as the parent of the same sex takes on that son's or daughter's feelings.

A third manner in which a boy or girl acquires his feeling of identity as masculine or feminine before school age is through a perception of what each of his parents does or does not do because of being a man or a woman.

We have pointed out that young children have quite definite ideas about the responsibilities and preferences of their fathers and mothers and are eager to fit in with the appropriate pattern. Households differ, of course. Each child will see the customs of his own home as "right," although he may tolerate different arrangements that he observes in the families of his playmates as being exceptions to the rule.

For example, in the Olins' household, the mother easily became discouraged and gloomy. She depended on her husband's more cheerful, buoyant approach to keep her on an even keel. Without realizing it, the Olin children early in life assumed that one facet of masculinity was a courageous, "every cloud has a silver lining," view of the world. How firm this impression had become was brought home to Mrs. Olin when she overheard her four-year-old daughter directing a play-mate. "You can be the daddy, and you must cheer me up, because I'm the mommy and everything is going wrong, and I'm going to cry."

In another family, the role of soother and en-courager might fall to the wife, resulting in quite a different perception of sex roles on the part of a young child. Still, the essential idea would be conveyed that mutual emotional support is part of a good relationship between a man and a woman.

Parental Behavior and the Identification Process

Let us push back a step further into the parental behavior that shapes masculinity and femininity. The child whose parent of the same sex tends to respond to situations in a manner considered typical for that sex gains in two ways, according to some studies. In observing typical masculine or feminine behavior much of the time, the youngster acquires, through identification, the confidence that he or she can master the necessary behavior. Then, when he or she goes to school and sees that his or her own actions and attitudes match quite well with the preferred behavior of his or her sex, a sense of being "all right" is strengthened.

If a mother or father does not display, or only rarely displays, characteristics typical for his or her sex, his son or her daughter may have less markedly typical characteristics. That may lead to the child's having doubts about his masculinity (or her femininity) as he or she encounters the more generally accepted behavior in contemporaries. Yet, in many families, the wife makes numerous important decisions without losing her essential femininity, without being an overpowering figure to her children or a threat to her husband. A working wife may still like being a woman and convey her satisfaction to her daughters, even when they are three, four, or five years old.

A husband need not be blustering and concerned with watching the ball game on TV or proving that he is in command in order to give his children the feeling of having the protection of a strong, responsible male. A gentle, mild-mannered father who has confidence in his manliness may be an excellent model for his sons. In other words, stereotyped behavior is not called for. Gratification in his or her sex membership on the part of a parent is as keenly felt, and as easily identified with, and probably more important than, outward behavior.

The Family Romance

Another vital phase of a small child's development

toward manhood or womanhood comes about through an attachment to the parent of the opposite sex during the preschool years. In Chapter 1 these years were described as a "rehearsal for adolescence." Nowhere is this rehearsal more apparent than in the way the small girl cuts her emotional teeth by trying out her feminine charms on Daddy, or the manner that little boys adopt toward their mothers, about whom they tend to be possessive and sometimes protective.

This special attachment to the parent of the opposite sex during these years is a step in the process of growing up. Like other steps, it is a healthy sign of an expanding personality. Also, like other steps or stages, this one needs to be worked through and then left behind. Usually around the age of six, if all has gone well, the boy who has been declaring, "I'm going to marry my mommy when I get bigger," or the girl who has been attempting to outmaneuver her mother in taking first place with daddy, decides that winning the parent of the opposite sex is a lost cause.

"Mommy and Daddy belong to each other," may have been only an unspoken precept, but it needs to, and usually does, get through to the preschooler. On an "If you can't beat 'em, join 'em" basis, boys ally themselves with their fathers and girls become closer to their mothers, about the time that they begin to shed their baby teeth. Unconsciously, or sometimes quite openly, they choose to be as much like the parent who did succeed in winning the desired object (that is, mother or father) as possible.

We may facilitate a youngster's progress through this phase of development if we accept it in a "Doesn't everybody?" manner. This is sometimes easier said than done. A little girl of three or four is so utterly endearing that her father may be tempted to want to keep her at just that convenient stage of adoration. He may even go along with her in pretending that she will replace her mother. He would do better to assure her that "Now you are my little girl, and Mommy is my wife. When you grow up, you'll be somebody's wife, too." A mother can hold out a similar hope to her son. "Boys like to think they want only their mommies. When you grow up you won't need me, and you'll find a wife for yourself, but we'll still be good friends."

A nice balance can be maintained, and is in most families, between undue encouragement of fantasies about getting rid of the parent of the same sex in order to obtain the one of the opposite sex for oneself, and making a child feel that his greater fondness for his mother, or for her father, is "bad" or a subject for ridicule. As in other situations, the best incentive a parent can offer a son or daughter is the viewpoint, "Growing up may mean giving up some things, but you'll find plenty of rewards to make up for what you leave behind as you grow." We can let a boy or girl know that others—perhaps we, too—once felt that only a father (or mother) would be the one we would love and want to spend all our time with, but that when we get older, we change our minds.

Parents Feel It, Too

Parents tend to feel especially drawn toward their three- to six-year-old offspring of the opposite sex, too. An interesting research study was carried on by Rothbart and Eleanor Maccoby (Maccoby is among the most respected of research designers):

> The parents were asked to react to a child's voice in a hypothetical situation. The recorded voice of a single child, which could not readily be identified as to sex, provided the stimulus material. Some of the parents were informed that it was a boy's voice, others that it was a girl's voice, and differences in the parents' reactions were then investigated. The results indicated that mothers tended to respond more permissively toward the boy's voice and fathers responded more permissively toward the girl's voice. An unexpected finding of this study was that mothers were more accepting of comfort-seeking in their sons than in their daughters.

For a woman dissatisfied in her own marriage, or for a man overly eager that his son be a "boy who can take it," this period of attachment to the parent of the opposite sex may hold a threat. Considerable security plus a robust sense of humor are called for to survive with unruffled temper when a three-year-old mischief-maker bedevils us all day and turns into an angel when her father walks through the door. Husbands can keep in mind that a weary, out-of-sorts wife can be reassured in countless ways. She may like to hear that a three-year-old has distinct limitations as a companion and that a wife really does come first.

It is only natural to be hurt and feel superfluous if a small daughter or son seems to be usurping the affections that are properly ours, especially if she or he is at the same time making heavy demands on us. If we see the situation in perspective and realize that it is only temporary, we will be far less likely to be resentful.

One-parent Families and Sexual Identity

With all the emphasis on the need for a parent of each sex at various times in the development of a youngster's confidence in himself or herself as a boy or as a girl, a parent who must bring up a son or a daughter without the presence of a mate may be discouraged about giving that child the opportunity for well-rounded development. A one-parent family is not necessarily an obstacle to a child's establishing adequate masculine or feminine identity. Single parents can still provide some companionship and models of the sex of the missing parent, but it may take extra thought and planning.

Those parents who have lived through the experience say that it is better to settle for being a good mother or an adequate father rather than feeling impelled to fill both roles. One will do better, too, by keeping in mind that thousands and thousands of competent, feminine women and masculine men grew up with only one parent in their childhood homes.

Grandparents are a "first line of support." A middle-aged grandfather can be an excellent masculine figure and model for a small boy or the man in a three- or four-year-old girl's life, even though Saturday afternoons with grandpa are less frequent than we might wish. Uncles, older cousins, the fathers of playmates, or middle-aged to elderly neighbors, far away from their own grandchildren, can also prove valuable in this capacity. A summer play-group for five-year-old boys run by older boys or men with teaching or camping experience can prove a good investment. Small girls without fathers need male companionship, too, and similar resources may be useful.

A woman keeping house alone for her children or sharing a home with another woman may need to make an effort to accept a certain amount of roughness and toughness from a son. One divorcee spoke bitterly of the "atmosphere of daintiness around here since there isn't a man in the house." Overvaluing quietness and good manners at the expense of more typically boyish behavior can work a hardship on young males.

A father left with small children to fend for needs a motherly person for both his girls and his boys, but out of sheer practical necessity, he is likely to have that in the person of a housekeeper. A woman with a young child of her own who lives in the house or brings her child to work with her can go a long way toward solving that problem. Housekeeping skills are far less important than warmth and patience with young children.

Usually, a man finds it easier to enlist another mother who will frequently include his child in excursions, peanut-butter-sandwich lunches, or rainy-day indoor play. Widowers are, in general, more fortunate than widows in that if they seek assistance from neighbors, wives of friends, or relatives they are not likely to be eyed with suspicion or rebuffed as intruders as a young woman might be.

Worries About Psychosexual Development

For most parents, helping young children feel that

both sexes are equally important and guiding them through the emotional and sexual development of these years is a far less pressing concern than working through situations involving nudity in the family, masturbation, or sex play between the children.

To adults who have become almost inured to seeing unclothed men and women on the screen and in the theater, modesty in the home might seem unnecessary. Then, too, many of us are still reacting strongly against the prudishness of an earlier day, which may have shadowed our own childhood. As was pointed out in the previous chapter, young children benefit by seeing other children of both sexes, who have not reached puberty, completely undressed. To observe that two, and only two, sexes exist, to have questions answered and doubts allayed is reassuring.

However, the sight of the adult nude body of one's own or of the opposite sex can have a different effect on the preschooler. The small girl who complained on seeing her mother without any clothes, "I'm so plain and you're so fancy," was voicing the discouragement about her own body that young children may feel on seeing adults unclad.

Such experiences may also be sexually stimulating, which can be even more disturbing to a preschooler. Three-, four- and five-year-olds are capable of sexual excitation. Although that *capacity* is a part of healthy development, habitual exposure to the sight of the nude adult body, or the practice of regularly taking baths or showers with a parent, may stir up more intense feeling than a youngster can deal with. This can make it difficult for the child to proceed comfortably to the next stage of development, which lasts from about six to the onset of puberty. During that stage, sexual feelings are far less prominent than in the preschool years, and energies, if all has gone well, are freed for becoming more reasonable, less demanding, and for achieving along many lines.

Certainly, parents are sometimes unnecessarily modest, too. Observing that adults use the toilet is one of the ways two- or two-and-a-half-year-olds learn about using it themselves. Once they have learned that lesson, they can learn that grown-ups sometimes like privacy and that even small children are entitled to it, too. If a youngster does burst in on a parent when he or she is undressed, no harm is done and surely no issue need be made of it. Yet continual parental nudity, for the sake of nudity, is hardly advisable even in today's world.

How Shall We Deal with Masturbation?

We need to take care that a boy or girl does not get the impression that parts of the body are not exposed because they are "not nice" or "shameful" or "dirty." That may be the preschooler's impression if too much, and too intense, stress is placed on modesty, especially if it is accompanied by disapproval of a young child's masturbating.

As a small person explores the world around him, he also explores his own body. Both boys and girls have been doing so since babyhood, as every parent has observed. Mothers and fathers are not likely to be upset by these explorations unless their own upbringing generated a high degree of guilt. Indeed, most parents today accept the fact that a preschool boy or girl may stroke his or her genital area when in need of comfort not immediately available in other ways.

Maria Piers, a noted child therapist and educator, says in her book *Growing Up With Children:*

Masturbation is a sign of development, just like cutting teeth, acquiring speech, or realizing how puzzles fit together. Like all these necessary steps, masturbation should be neither artificially rushed, nor stimulated, nor greatly discouraged when it does occur. After all, what a child should learn is not that relief of sexual tensions is evil, but that it should not take place in public. The capacity for adult sexual enjoyment does not emerge all of a sudden in early adulthood. Like all human capacities, it develops step by step. Masturbation is the first step.

Excessive guilt over masturbation can be damaging. The preschool child, for reasons that will be explained in the following chapter, often feels guilty in many situations, out of all proportion to what he has done or to the reproof his parents have given him. Children sense that anything related to sexuality, although they may never have heard the word, has a special meaning for adults. If we need to say to a child who has been embarrassing us by masturbating in front of strangers, as a shy, uneasy youngster is likely to do, "You may do that when you are alone, but not when other people are around," we can take care to keep the tone as casual as possible.

If masturbation seems excessive—that is, a youngster appears to be driven to it frequently throughout the day—it may be a sign that he or she is lonely, unhappy, or troubled by feelings of guilt and/or of being unloved and unlovable. If a new baby has come into the family or some other sharp change in a three- or four-year-old's surroundings has occurred, he may need extra reassurance and comfort. The question to be resolved is not how to put a stop to masturbation, but rather how to meet the child's needs more effectively so that his energies can be freed for other activities.

Perhaps such a child needs more affectionate attention and approval from his parents, more companionship with others his age, standards that are not so high that living up to them is a strain. Some thought about and experimenting with the arrangements of his daily life may be necessary to discover the cause of his being troubled.

If a parent is not aware whether his three- or four-year-old is masturbating after he has been tucked in bed, he should not feel he must find out in order to be a good parent.

Sex Play Among Young Children

One other manifestation of a young child's sexuality that disturbs parents is sex play among children. Almost every preschooler at some time takes part in explorations with other children that might be considered "sex play." If such activities are persistent, we may need to deal with the situation directly in ways that will be discussed. Threats or punishments are no solution. The most helpful attitude on the part of parents is to keep calm and avoid appearing shocked or devastated. To declare that such play is "dirty," "bad," or "shameful" serves no purpose.

A frequent occurrence among the three-year-olds is episodes of undressing. A youngster who is worried about the difference between boys and girls, or not sure whether all boys and all girls have the same genital equipment, may persuade his or her playmates to take off their clothes. If we find our son or daughter involved in such incidents, we will need to make sure he feels he can bring any questions he has to us, even though we may have believed we had already cleared up his or her doubts. To stop the play we might say something like, "We undress when we go to bed or when we take a bath or change our clothes. Other times we keep our clothes on. Taking them off when you are playing is sort of babyish. Lots of children try it once, but you are big enough to know that we don't get undressed outdoors or take off our clothes while we're playing."

The delicate question of whether to report such incidents to the mothers of the other children involved depends somewhat on how we think they will react and how friendly we are with them. One woman found her five-year-old and his two four-year-old friends undressed and playing "going to bed together." She had dealt with the situation calmly by firmly announcing, "We always keep our clothes on when we're playing, in the house or outside, and we'll find something that is a better game than that."

Afterward, she and her husband discussed reporting the incident to the parents of the other children. They decided that one set of parents would probably be extremely upset, or else blame the episode entirely on the five-year-old and forbid their child to see him any more, so that saying nothing would be wisest. As for the other set of parents, with whom they were on good terms and who they felt would undoubtedly take a reasonable view of the children's behavior, they agreed to give that couple an account of what had occurred and how it had been handled.

Some perfectly "nice" children experiment with mutual masturbation once or twice. It is not always the bad influence of "the other children" that is responsible, nor are boys rather than girls, or the slightly older rather than the younger of the children, necessarily the initiators. Keeping that fact in mind may help us refrain from fixing blame on a particular child or predicting a dire future for the suspected instigator.

If we find two or three children involved in sexual activities, we may need to supervise them and keep them supplied with materials and ideas that are sufficiently challenging and enjoyable so that sex play will not be their chief attraction for one another. "Supervision" does not mean that we need be suspicious every time those youngsters are playing together quietly, or that we question a son or daughter about exactly what the two have been doing.

If one boy's or girl's playmates really do seem to be preoccupied with sexual exploration, we may need to provide other playmates. If a child has a number of interests, he or she may be relieved to have us say, "Let's get Dave and his sister over here this afternoon. I think you and Herbie are getting tired of just being together with each other all the time." If we can discourage rather than forbid association with the offending Herbie, we avoid making him attractive just because his company is taboo. We also thus give the child the support he may require to remove himself from Herbie, for whose company he may have no desire.

Unless a youngster is experiencing an overwhelming conflict over feelings about the difference between males and females, or allied questions, he will usually respond to other kinds of play and other playmates. If parents believe their youngster has a deeper problem, they may want to consult a child-guidance clinic or child therapist.

Looking Toward the Youngster's Adulthood

If our goal is to guide our child toward a firm conviction that his own sex and his feelings about it are acceptable, and that the opposite one is also equally "all right," we are giving him good support in his efforts to grow up. We can work toward that goal through our presentation of the roles of men and of women in many facets of daily life and through the way we respond to a youngster's attachment to the parent of the opposite sex during these years. Then we may reasonably look forward to our boy or girl becoming an adult with a capacity to enjoy a full and satisfactory sexual relationship—no slight achievement.

7
Toward a Healthy Conscience

"ONSCIENCE DOTH MAKE cowards of us all," said Hamlet. We would all agree that conscience makes us cautious and prudent in many circumstances, and often conforming. Yet it is more than the regulator of "middle-class morality," as Hamlet implies. If the foundations for responsible behavior have been laid down in the early years, conscience may also impel the more mature individual to stand up for his beliefs even when that might entail risking discomfort or unpopularity.

How does a healthy conscience develop? What pulls and tensions undergird it, and what causes it to become troublesomely overactive? What attitudes and teaching on the part of parents make for a useful, working conscience?

Although the actions of the three- through five-year-old do not continually evidence, in conventional ways, how busy his conscience is, an understanding of its operations and its limitations is often the key to his behavior, both the desirable and the less desirable variety.

How Does Conscience Grow?

A boy or girl develops a serviceable conscience as he makes the customs and values of his family, his neighborhood, and his culture into his own inner monitor. The serviceable preschool conscience is one that asserts itself when actions, forbidden or dangerous, need to be stopped but does not exert such intense pressures or impose such severe restrictions that it interferes with the enjoyment of daily living.

The inner monitor develops through a youngster's relationships with other people whom he loves, depends on, and takes as models. Their approval or disapproval, in words and actions, cultivates it and its accompanying sense of guilt. Some capacity to feel guilt is essential to acquiring the restraints necessary to becoming a socialized human being, as emphasized earlier in this volume.

When a preschooler experiences appropriate guilt over wrongdoing, his feelings range from uncomfortable to miserable. Those feelings are one of the forces deterring him from repeating unacceptable behavior.

Through the growth of conscience come those ethical values of honesty, respect, and concern for the rights of others, including their possessions, and an understanding of why rules and laws are necessary and why we obey them even when it is inconvenient to do so.

Parents instill such values through the manner in which they handle situations in their own lives, which small children observe, often unwittingly. Values are also brought home to the young by the approval or disapproval they receive for their own behavior. If a high value is set on spontaneous helpfulness and consideration, on behaving honorably even when "nobody is looking," on generosity, on the observance of the spirit, not simply the letter, of the law, a child tends to develop a social conscience. That is more to be aimed at as a goal than mere obedience.

Conscience Takes on a "Local Color"

Clearly, different societies, different groups within each society, and different periods in history have labeled various actions as "good" or "bad." As a result, children grow up with inner monitors that make widely differing demands on them. An extreme example of such a variation is the legend of the Spartan boy who stole a fox and let it gnaw his flesh away as he carried it stoically under his cloak. Stealing and suffering pain in silence were, in the ethics of military Sparta, 2,500 years ago, exemplary conduct. A child who did either, or both at once, could live at peace with his conscience. We may assume that some Spartan children were often troubled because they were failing to live up to the painful and unchildlike standards held up for them.

Most children in the late twentieth-century United States are taught a set of values of another kind. Not only stealing, but concealing a serious wound, would result in disapproval from responsible adults.

Conscience Grows Step by Step

Let us see how the values we are trying to establish come, eventually, to take hold. One of the first prohibitions a child comes up against when he can get around under his own power is that he must not tamper with certain objects under any circumstances, nor with some others unless he has been given permission to touch them. In the first category might be the jars and colored sticks in his mother's makeup box, matches, his father's razor, or the earth in the flower pot on the windowsill. Among objects that may be handled or taken with permission might be the occasional piece of candy in a candy dish, the switches and buttons on the TV, the radio, the telephone, or an older brother's or sister's favorite toy.

Long before she was three, Jean had learned to stay away from certain "No-no's" if and when one of her parents or her older sister was within sight and gave a warning, "Not for Jean." That was an advance over having to be separated from the forbidden object in spite of verbal reminders. After a few more months, Jean would stay away from a forbidden object as long as someone representing authority was present; she no longer required an admonition in words.

Between her third and fourth birthdays, Jean went through a stage of walking up to the candy box, or the control buttons on the TV set, or her mother's makeup box, looking around to see if anyone could observe her, and then solemnly saying, "Not for Jeanie," but succumbing to temptation anyway. She had a budding but unreliable conscience. After she had gained a bit more control, her own warning to herself was usually effective.

A year or so later her conscience was operating automatically, at least in the matter of decorating her face with lipstick. Stuffing it with licorice drops was another story. That temptation took longer for her conscience to conquer.

Different children attain a reliable conscience at different ages. One that is reliable in one situation may still be shaky or nonexistent in many others. For Jean, keeping away from her mother's lipstick seemed to become easier as she began to enjoy using crayons and paper, but it still consumed so much of her reservoir of resistance that, when confronted with other "No-no's," she needed the support of the sight, if not the voice, of one of her elders.

Vacillation is to be expected. The preschooler's conscience is similar to one of those microscopic forms of life that after bulging in one direction tend to shrink in another.

Encouraging a Realistic Inner Monitor

Jean's parents had aided the development of their daughter's inner controls through reasonably consistent discipline (discussed in Chapter 4). For example, if the little girl was spoken to sternly on one occasion for smearing her mother's eye shadow all over her face, she was not applauded as "the cutest thing in the world" the next time she tried it. They had also geared their teaching to Jean's level of understanding and temperament.

Her parents had been generous with encouragement when Jean demonstrated that she could take responsibility for observing the regulations prevailing

in the household and when she played outdoors with other children or went to their homes. From her earliest days, most of the adults with whom she came in contact let her know that they had faith in her ability to take a new step and to become more grown-up in her behavior. Mistakes she made along the way were not interpreted as a sign that she was clumsy, uncooperative, or willful. "You are the kind who can do it," "Jean is a girl who does her best," were attitudes that prevailed in her home generally. Even when her mother's or father's patience wore thin, the warmth she usually received tided her over.

Such an atmosphere clearly sets up the boundaries of acceptable behavior. It also lessens the burden of uneasy guilt some children carry because they do not know where they stand or because they lack the satisfaction of believing they can please the adults they love.

Conscience Can Prompt Considerate Behavior

The development of a healthy conscience is facilitated, too, by the example of adults who, without preaching about doing so, carry out their responsibilities and are not in the habit of "trying to get away with something."

An inner monitor that demands consideration for the feelings and needs of others most of the time, as well as prompting observance of the rules, grows out of seeing and identifying with the considerate behavior of a parent or another adult the child loves.

For instance, a father preparing supper for his four-year-old, in a wife's absence, breaks her favorite dish or burns her most useful cooking pan. When his wife returns, he tells her he is sorry about the damage and then carefully glues together the dish or painstakingly scours the pan. A small child witnessing this and other kinds of considerate behavior gets the idea that hurting, offending, or disappointing someone is as much to be deplored as breaking a definite rule. Gradually, as he absorbs the meaning of consideration, his inner monitor will prompt him to help when someone needs assistance.

Right and Wrong Appear Differently with Age

Not all manifestations of a child's conscience coincide with adult values. Small children, in their efforts to cope with a confusing world and their own feelings, often have a "bad conscience" over trivial or nonexistent misdemeanors. Indeed, they may be vocally hypercritical of the behavior of anyone who errs by doing what they themselves have only recently acquired sufficient control not to do (discussed in the section on "Tattling" in Chapter 3).

A four- or five-year-old can be tiresomely self-righteous over details and oblivious to the larger issues his parents have been trying to teach.

An extreme example of such confusion of values is depicted in Richard Hughes's *A High Wind in Jamaica*, that bizarre tale of mid-nineteenth-century children. The ship on which their parents have placed them to return to England from their remote island home is captured by pirates. The children live for several months with the pirates in the midst of lawlessness, seduction, piracy, and murder. "Grown-ups never *do* tell us things," they say to one another when events become incomprehensible. They quickly accommodate themselves to life on the pirate ship, delighted with being permissively treated.

Eventually they are reunited with their parents in England and the pirates are captured and brought to trial. The children are taken to the office of the family solicitor to give their testimony. There this conversation takes place:

The solicitor asked, "When you were with these men, did they ever do anything you didn't like? You know what I mean, something *nasty?*"

"Yes!" cried Rachel. . . . "He talked about drawers," she said in a shocked voice.

"What did he say?"

"He told us once not to toboggan down the deck on them. . . ." That comment came from Emily, who was ten, but her five-year-old sister, Rachel, added, "He shouldn't have talked about drawers."

Granted these were children of the Victorian era, but the basic paradox is much the same today. Conscience, in its early phases, tends to fasten on trivialities and fails to comprehend broader issues of right and wrong, honesty and dishonesty.

Parents Can Side with Conscience

When a boy or girl, with disproportionate guilt and anxiety, tells us that he has called someone a "bad name," or walked across the neighbor's grass, or broken a cup that was already cracked, we may be so relieved that nothing worse took place that we laugh and take a "think nothing of it" attitude.

We help a youngster most if we can diminish his guilt yet take the side of conscience. Something to the effect that, "I know you feel sorry, and it's O.K. Everyone forgets (or makes a mistake, or drops things) sometimes. Now that you've told me about it, you'll feel better," is a statement that supports conscience. Punctuated with a hug and a kiss, such a statement does not add to a youngster's troubles by asking him to feel he has been hopelessly foolish.

"True" and "False" Sometimes Blur

For a small child to separate the "real" from the "pretend" is often all but impossible. Take the difficult plight of Tony, an intensely imaginative three-and-a-half-year-old who lived in a home where pets were talked to and treated almost as if they were human. Oscar was a highly intelligent German shepherd dog, who, to dog lovers, appeared to comprehend and respond to anything that was said to him. Oscar had been Tony's companion and guardian since babyhood. One day Tony was not to be found for several hours. His frantic mother had just summoned his father home from work when a nonchalant Tony walked in. He had gone to the home of a new friend several blocks away to play. When his mother reminded him, in the course of a stern rebuke, that he had often been told never to go farther than the corner without asking permission, he replied, "But I asked Oscar, and he knew where I was all the time."

Tony suffered no pangs of conscience as a result

of this escapade, since in his limited understanding of the distinction between the real and the imaginary, Oscar, the dog, was as qualified to give permission as any human being. Tony was neither alibiing nor pretending. This was a case of faulty comprehension. Even patient explanations on the part of his parents of the limitations of a dog's understanding made scant impression on him. Tony's vivid imagination made it more difficult to help him separate his make-believe world from the real one in many instances.

"But I do *so* know what Oscar means when he talks to me, and he knows what I say to him, too. You're always telling people how smart Oscar is, but you don't understand him yourself," was Tony's position.

Often a preschooler's statement that appears to adults or even to older children to be a falsehood merely reflects a lack of vocabulary. Four-year-olds who can count to six or even to ten may not take the trouble to do so and will therefore report an incident in exaggerated form. Three fire engines in front of the apartment house on the corner may be parlayed into "millions" or "lots and lots of fire engines, all the way down the street."

Even, "I only took two weeny, tiny, baby cookies," does not always indicate an absence of conscience or a dangerous tendency to prevarication, when the supply of cookies in the jar has clearly been diminished by half a dozen or more.

Helping a Youngster Toward Truthfulness

When a three- or four- or five-year-old has committed some offense that seems to him likely to bring him into parental disfavor, he may construct an elaborate but flimsy tale of why he "just had to do that," or deny altogether that he was involved in the affair, or put the blame for it on another person. Such conduct is quite typical of preschoolers and not to be regarded as a serious lack of feeling for right and wrong, as one might judge it to be in an older boy or girl.

We help a child become more truthful in owning up to a misdeed by not making it seem that he is hopelessly disgraced or by not meting out too severe a punishment when he tells us about it. "Next time you'll find a better way. I don't think you'll want to do that again," or "It would have been better to . . . ," or "I know you feel bad over what happened, and you'll get along better if you don't try that again," are attitudes that accomplish several important aims.

Such an approach lets a child know that telling a parent about his wrongdoing will not make him an outcast. It also lets him know how to avoid similar mishaps in the future and affirms our faith that he *can* do better. That in itself encourages both acceptable conduct and the ability to own up to slips. Since confession is good for the soul and tends to relieve painful guilt, the child who is able to report his peccadilloes without being made to feel worthless is having a healthy experience.

"Chris seemed to feel so guilty and so sure he would be severely punished," said a father in discussing some childish mischief his son had been involved in, "that we really thought we ought to give him the severe punishment he expected."

Although confession need not guarantee immunity from any penalty, the line of reasoning taken by Chris's father can make a young conscience too sensitive, if it is followed habitually. A parent knows better than a four- or five-year-old just how serious a misdeed is and how it should be handled.

In the interest of developing a realistic, not a rigid, inner monitor, parents can certainly trust their own judgment, not the youngster's estimate of the enormity of his "badness."

Avoiding Impasses

We can often avoid an impasse over truthfulness by preventing situations in which untruthfulness would be all too easy. Children tend to give the answer they think we would like to hear, or one that would let them off of some disagreeable task.

If a four-year-old is sent to wash her hands and she comes back seemingly as grimy as ever, the answer to "Did you really wash carefully?" will undoubtedly be affirmative. Maybe she did wash, in sketchy fashion. Maybe she did not even make the attempt because the hot water is so hot, or the faucet is so hard to reach, or she is afraid she will miss something if she stays away long enough to do a thorough job. She then compounds her carelessness with a falsehood. Better not put the question! We know the answer, anyway.

We have the choice of sending her back to do the job satisfactorily or accepting her performance, but to ask for an honest answer, when truthfulness would result in inconvenience, is putting too great a temptation in a small child's path.

The Wish Is Sometimes Father to the Falsehood

Children deviate from the facts for a variety of other reasons. One who feels deprived of affection or companionship, who craves recognition, or longs for a certain toy, may reveal that desire in "tall tales" told to his playmates or the neighbors. In his stories, the absent or totally inadequate father becomes the generous or powerful figure who grants every wish and can do "just about anything." The pet a boy or girl daydreams about owning, or the baby sister a five-year-old girl fantasies would be company for her, are represented as already being members of the household, often to the great embarrassment of parents.

One small boy, whose family lived in an apartment house where pets were prohibited, was so factual in his description of the big, white "Lassie-dog" he owned that the landlord threatened his parents with eviction. "Either you are liars or your kid is," this irate gentleman insisted. "If it's the kid, he should be walloped, and if it's you, out you go. That kid has made trouble for me with the other tenants with his stories about the dog you keep locked in the bathroom."

The parents explained to their son that when he talked about his "Lassie-dog," he should be sure to say it was a "pretend dog." The interest with which the neighbors had listened to his account of the details of keeping his dog in the apartment had been so gratifying to the boy that he was loath to relinquish the attention that ownership of a dog had brought him.

When a small boy or girl is quite obviously weaving a story that is pure fabrication, we can help him by saying, "That's a good 'pretend story,' but you and

I know it's just for pretending, don't we?" In that way we anchor the youngster to reality, yet do not brand his imaginings as "lies." We can point out frequently, in various contexts, the difference between make-believe and fact without branding a four-year-old as untrustworthy. This question is discussed from other angles in Chapter 5.

When Conscience Generates Fantasy

Especially hard for parents to handle is a child's report of an event that might be a figment of his imagination invented to secure an end of his own, or might be true—and serious. That was the dilemma in which Claire's parents found themselves. Claire was an imaginative four-and-a-half-year-old. Like many youngsters her age, she was afraid of the dark and would go to almost any lengths to get one of her parents to stay with her if she woke during the night.

One morning she told a most convincing tale of "the Honey Man, an extra big man, carrying a real big bag, all blue all over with a funny thing over his face," who had entered her room during the night, walked around, and then departed by the window through which he had come. Since the family lived on the first floor of a two-story building, the idea that the ground-level windows were an invitation to prowlers had often crossed the parents' minds. Had they, they wondered, said anything in their daughter's hearing to suggest that?

When Claire was asked if she had seen this man put anything in his bag, she replied, "No. He just hunted around. The bag was for honey."

"Why didn't you call us if somebody was in your room? You call often enough for nothing at all," said her father, trying to be casual.

"The Honey Man didn't need you. He said he'd come back later if he wanted to see you." Whatever else she might be, the little girl was not at a loss for answers.

Her perplexed parents settled for telling Claire she had probably dreamed that the Honey Man had been in her room, since nothing in the house had been taken. On the off chance that a potential burglar or molester had been in the girl's room, it seemed unfair to accuse her of fabrication. Yet accepting her story and acceding to her wish to have either mother or father sleep with her, or to be permitted to sleep with them, would make it clear that her parents were worried about her safety, and it was not advisable for other reasons.

Magical Thinking

Another and deeper cause for Claire's fantasy, for fantasy it probably was, may have been an overactive conscience. To children, thinking about doing something "bad" seems as dangerous and as likely to bring punishment as carrying out the deed. They do not distinguish, for instance, between wanting to get rid of baby brother and actually throwing him out of the window.

As has been pointed out, children (like most primitive peoples) attribute magical powers to their thoughts. If an illness or a mishap occurs to a person for whom they wished "something bad" or with whom they are temporarily angry, they may hold themselves accountable for the misfortune and suffer keenly.

Sometimes an explanation of the difference between wishing or thinking something "bad" and doing something "bad" reassures a child and eases his primitive conscience. Such an explanation may need to be made more than once.

As a result of his wishes or his thoughts, a child may anticipate that punishment will descend on him, perhaps in the shape of a witch or an ogre, a large animal, or a strange person like Claire's Honey Man, who comes at night when a small boy or girl is alone and defenseless. Such is the genesis of many unreal fears during the years from three to six, and for that matter, in later childhood. In an unconscious effort to get rid of the fears caused by his overactive—or misguided—conscience, the child often resorts to elaborate and restrictive rituals, which may become so all-pervasive as to interfere with play, with undertaking new experiences or finding much relish in daily living.

Ritual Routines Allay Fear

One four-year-old had instituted bedtime routines including a story, a goodnight song from his father, putting on pajamas and then slippers and robe—always in that order—collecting five toys to take to bed, which must be arranged in a particular way, plus further ceremonies that became a burden to his parents. Following the exact pattern every night at bedtime gave him some relief from his fears that a monster would come up from the basement and devour him.

No matter how kind and gentle the adults around him may be, a youngster may develop a troublesome conscience. He is alarmed by his own impulses to strike out or be violent. These he is learning to deal with during his preschool years, or at least not to act on. Yet even as his actions come under control, the wish to hit out aggressively, the frightening anger, persist within him. Daydreams of glory through aggressions, if they do not take over completely, may be a safety valve. Imaginary companions who take on either human or animal guise, or a doll or stuffed animal, may be a means of displacing or enforcing, as circumstances require, the restrictions that conscience sets up.

Miss Beibler was the imaginary friend of four-year-old Alicia. Miss Beibler needed to be constantly reproved, reformed, and redirected. "You don't know how bad Miss Beibler'd be if I didn't scold her real hard. Sometimes I even have to spank her and make her stay home when we are going somewhere, 'cause she does such naughty things," Alicia would tell her mother. Through the wicked Miss Beibler, Alicia was getting rid of, or "displacing," some of the guilt her conscience imposed on her, although she had no idea Miss B. was serving so complicated a purpose. In rebuking Miss B., Alicia was also taming her own tendencies toward wildness.

Such a means of disposing of uncomfortable guilt over fancied wrongdoing is a step on the path toward a healthy conscience, a conscience that will in time make itself felt in more useful ways.

Conscience Can Create Worries Over Sex

In the previous chapter, the desire of the preschooler to have the parent of the opposite sex for himself was explained as a part of normal emotional development. Yet this wish, too, can result in distressing pangs of conscience. In a small girl, conflict often arises over her wish to get the better of her mother, since this is at odds with her conviction that mother is far from expendable. Small boys who would like to have their mother's entire attention are often disturbed because they still admire and want to be like those rivals for mother's affection, their fathers. Conscience may then become acutely bothersome in some children.

A small child who has engaged in sex play or even thought about doing so, or who has been severely reprimanded for masturbating, may have a guilty conscience that threatens him with all manner of dreadful punishments. A boy may fear that his penis will fall off or be cut off as punishment. A girl may imagine that she once had a penis but lost it because she was "bad."

Such troublesome consciences are less likely to beset youngsters whose questions about sex differences and about human reproduction have been answered. One who knows he may bring his worries to his parents without either being rebuffed or having to listen to an incomprehensible lecture on biology may be spared unnecessary worries arising from guilt.

Almost all children suffer some guilt over worries related to sex, whether or not their parents give them any basis for such worries. A parent has not failed a son or daughter if such worries come to light. See the previous two chapters and the following one for further discussion of these questions.

"Mine" and "Yours" Are Difficult Concepts

A conscience that deters a youngster from taking

things that do not belong to him develops slowly, and again through example. Here we may need to do some soul-searching about our own ethics. To take an object belonging to another is not countenanced by most parents if that "other" is an individual. But what about reminding the bus driver that he has not collected our fare? Or getting a thirteen-year-old into the movies at half-price when twelve is the age for paying adult admission? Or taking an ashtray, a spoon, or a towel from a motel? Family morals may veer to a double standard. Some children get the feeling from their parents' behavior that it would be wrong to cheat Mr. Grimozzi who owns the grocery store on the corner, yet cheating a faceless corporation of a few cents or a few furnishings is all right. "They will never miss it anyway," or "At the rate they charge you, they expect it."

Unless we stay with the doctrine that under no circumstances does one take what is not his, no matter whom it belongs to, we can hardly be surprised if the younger members of the family bring home in their pockets assorted crayons, doll dishes, or small cars from nursery school or from the homes of playmates.

One expects a certain amount of this from three- and four-year-olds. They are often as unaware of the implications of taking what is not theirs as they are of the difference between fact and fantasy in the stories they relate. Conscience expands and becomes increasingly serviceable as we help them, gently, to distinguish between honesty and dishonesty.

Willy was a five-year-old who constantly brought home small treasures such as colored pencils, pieces of candy, crayons, and trinkets. When questioned as to where he got them, he replied that he had "found" them. At first his parents paid scant attention to his peculiar luck. They did not want to accuse him of "swiping" these items, and they dismissed his behavior as "just a phase." Willy had often heard his older brothers say "Finders keepers, losers weepers" about objects left around the house. This misleading catchword may have contributed to Willy's easygoing conscience.

Taking Corrective Measures

Willy's father, unable to close his eyes any longer to his son's taking ways, said to him, "Willy, everything belongs to someone. At kindergarten I know there is a lost-and-found box. Anything you find on the playground or in your kindergarten room or on the way to school belongs in that box in the school office, so the person it belongs to can get it. When you are at a friend's house you never, never ask to have or help yourself to a toy or picture book or anything else that is theirs."

"Well, sometimes kids give me things because they like me. That's how I got those crayons, even if you don't think I did," Willy asserted stoutly.

"People may like you a lot, Willy, and I'm sure they do like you, but they don't give you their toys and other possessions. You've gotten a little mixed up, I'm afraid," his father told him.

"Well," said Willy, thoughtfully, "Those old picture books I just borrowed from some of my friends. I can tell them tomorrow I borrowed them."

"You don't 'borrow' something without asking your friend's mother if you may borrow it, and then you take it back real soon. I think what you and I better do right now is to take those picture books back to the boys you borrowed them from and say you want them to have them back."

Willy reluctantly made the rounds of the homes of the three friends from whom he had "borrowed" the picture books without asking permission to do so. His father made it easier for him by going along and doing some of the explaining.

Willy's parents also kept a close watch on what Willy brought home. If he came home with a miniature car or two that he claimed he had found, they refrained from asking "Where did you get it?," as that might have only opened the way to further falsehoods. They just saw to it that the toy was returned, without shaming or punishing Willy.

His father might say, "Willy, I believe you forgot about not picking up a friend's toys and putting them in your pocket. Until you can remember for yourself, your mother and I will help you by reminding you that you take those cars back to the friend they belong to. You can't take things that aren't yours. People don't like it if you do. We have to be able to trust the people around us, to be sure that they won't take things away from us that are ours. And you know something, Willy? I think you'll feel a lot better after those cars have been returned." Since Willy's conscience was still so shaky, his parents acted for that dormant conscience, although they never spoke of their watchfulness in such terms.

Had Willy been three rather than five, his parents might justifiably have been less insistent on his making restitution. Had he been three or four years older than he was, they might, also with good reason, have felt Willy needed help from a child-guidance clinic. Most children around the age of five or six do some "swiping." That, in itself, is not a sign that they will continue to steal or become delinquents, but it is a sign that until conscience becomes stronger, they need firm reminders.

Indirect Support for the Chronic "Swiper"

If parents have a youngster like Willy, they can help him, in addition to acting as a monitor until his inner one can take over, by not regarding him as a thief. As with any other behavior lapse, a child is helped most by feeling that those around him, especially his parents, have confidence that he can overcome his problem.

Some older children steal because they feel unloved. They are, in effect, not stealing an object they want as much as they are trying to get, by hook or by crook, the love they feel they have been denied. This kind of stealing is usually confined to older children, but it may enter also into the chronic "swiping" of the five-year-old. The child who has a tendency to take what belongs to someone else needs plenty of affection and a life with satisfactions in it. Parents need to take care not to let their unavoidable concern, embarrassment, or worry over stealing color their entire relationship with a youngster.

Such a youngster is also helped to understand property rights if his own belongings are protected from the depredations of other members of the family. Mothers may need to think twice before, in an excess of zeal for neatness, they throw out a four- or five-year-old's "junk." Nor do we allow a younger brother or sister to wreak havoc on an older one's carefully constructed, if crude, skyscraper, or the bits of knotted cloth a girl calls her "babies."

Probably no one measure in itself can expand conscience during these years to the point at which it will always be strong enough to resist the temptation to appropriate another's possession, especially when no one is looking. Occasional lapses will most likely occur. A combination of example, building up self-respect, and supplying sufficient affection and adventure so that the preschooler does not fall into the habit of "swiping" out of sheer boredom—plus a firm insistence on the return of any articles mysteriously "found"—will usually, in time and with patience, yield a reliable conscience. When conscience becomes active enough, and a boy or girl is uncomfortable over having made off with goods to which he or she has no right, the tendency to "find" or "swipe" or "just borrow" with no intention of returning will gradually fade out in most cases.

Parents may be encouraged when they realize that conscience does not flower through severity or solemn pronouncements on their part. Their youngster's unfolding confidence in himself as a worthwhile person, one who can take the right action and one who has their love and approval, is a basic ingredient for progress toward a healthy conscience. Consistent guidance, attainable standards, and protection from overwhelming and frequent temptations will also aid the development of an inner monitor, which, although faltering at times, over the long haul steadily steers the growing boy or girl into more responsible and responsive behavior.

8

Fears

ALL YOUNG CHILDREN at some times know fear, and
each finds his own style of dealing with it. A wide
range of feelings and behavior are included in the term
fear. The child who stays behind the railing bordering
the tiger's cage at the zoo and does not put his hand
through the bars because he is afraid of being bitten is
showing sensible caution. If he were so afraid of the
tiger that he refused to look at him, he would be suffering from a groundless fear, sometimes called a phobia.
If any mention of a family excursion sent the youngster
into a state of panic lest the outing involve going to
the zoo, he would be suffering from acute anxiety, or
disabling anticipation of danger or misfortune.

Helen Ross, in her pamphlet *Fears of Children,*
says:

Both fear and courage are a part of each of us, both
are ways of feeling, both belong to our efforts to

master a situation. But fear is probably harder to understand than courage.

Our consideration of the fears of the preschooler covers three areas: the sources of worry and terror; the children's ways of defending themselves against those feelings; and some steps parents can take that may help their offspring to cope with their fears, be they real or imagined, present or in the future.

Some Fear Is Inevitable

Conscientious fathers and mothers have sometimes tried to create a "fear-proof" existence for their children. Yet, in spite of their preparing a youngster in advance for unsettling events, in spite of their pooh-poohing those villains of fairy tale and legend, the witches and ogres, their children in their preschool years have been subject to unwarranted fears, such as fear of going down the drain with the bath water, or of encountering monsters who spring out of doorways.

The most loving parents cannot completely protect a child from apprehension about unreal dangers as well as actual ones. Although disquietude sometimes comes from outside pressures, some of it also comes from inner turmoil and has no visible or perceptible source. A child's well-being depends, as Selma Fraiberg points out in *The Magic Years:*

. . . not on the presence or absence of ogres in his fantasy life, or on such fine points as the diet of ogres. *It depends upon the child's solution to the ogre problem.*

It is the way in which a child manages his irrational fears that determines their effect upon his personality development. . . . Normally the child overcomes his irrational fears. . . . If we understand the nature of the developing child and those parts of his personality that work for solution and resolution toward mental health, we are in the best position to assist him in developing his inner resources for dealing with fears.

To understand the genesis of fear, we need to go back to the first year of life. When an infant is uncomfortable because he is hungry, cold, or soaking wet, because he hears a loud noise, or too strong a light is shining in his eyes, he responds with his entire body. If he is hungry, he is hungry "all over." He screams, he waves his arms and legs around and behaves as someone might in a state of utter panic. His discomfort is so disagreeable that after he has felt it a number of times, at its first sign he anticipates with dread what will follow. He has learned fear. If the disagreeable experience occurs too often, he will have learned anxiety as well.

Fear, depending on its degree and the personality of the child involved, may be a help or a hindrance to growth and survival. Caution, a mild and essential byproduct of fear, seems to be acquired spontaneously by some children.

Yet, not all youngsters understand the need for caution. "The burned child fears the fire" is a glib proverb that does not always hold true. The three-year-old often has too hazy a notion of cause and effect to connect his behavior logically with its painful results.

To understand that whatever has hurt him is an impersonal agent, neither malevolent in its attack on him nor punitive, takes a certain amount of maturity.

Too Fearless for His Own Good

A three-year-old, who had paid no heed to any teaching about safety in crossing streets, was hit by a car. He was not badly hurt, miraculously, but he did have to spend a few days in the hospital. His father explained to him that the car had hit him because he had run into its path and the driver could not stop in time to avoid him. Now, maybe he would remember why people must watch out for automobiles, cross only at street corners, etc., etc. To the father's amazement, the boy had no memory of having run into the street, but insisted he was on the sidewalk when "that automobile came after me." Probably the shock had been so great that the actual circumstances had been erased from the child's mind, but in any case, his experience was not a useful lesson.

A bad experience with real danger will not necessarily teach caution. At best, having been frightened is only one side of learning discretion. A child acquires a sensible attitude toward danger as he becomes sufficiently mature to see the relationship, for instance, between leaning over the windowsill and losing his balance and falling out, or putting an object in an electric socket and getting a shock. He acquires caution, also, as he makes his parents' admonitions a part of himself, a process discussed in the previous chapter.

Those youngsters who repeatedly jump from heights too great for a safe landing, who will not keep away from fire, who are reckless about running into the street, who seemingly disregard parental instruction about safety altogether when they are three and a half or four, may be testing their own power to make everything come out all right. They may indulge in an undue amount of magic thinking about their own or their parents' omnipotence.

The four-and-a-half-year-old girl who declared, "I can climb the highest tree in the world and I won't get hurt if I fall out of it, because my father is a doctor," was·bemused by her own wish for, or perhaps fear of, a father who was extremely protective or powerful. Perhaps, too, she was testing his as well as her own ability to control events by climbing higher than prudence would dictate.

A Mask for Anxiety

The three-year-old who, time after time, gets himself into offbeat and dangerous situations is not as likely to be without fear as to be driven by anxiety about some disturbing situation in his life. His anxiety may arise from tension in the atmosphere of his home. He may have been alarmed by arguments he has heard between his parents that he could not understand, questions that he hesitated to ask or that his parents did not answer. These or other causes may push him to explore and experiment in bizarre or forbidden ways.

Then there is the three- or three-and-a-half-year-old who shows no signs of fear of events or phenomena that usually alarm others his age. Thunder, the dark, frisky, barking dogs, or separation from adults who are important to him seem to make no impression on him.

If, in addition, such a child is rather listless, lacking in the usual childlike zest for play, if his emotional life seems flat and toneless, or his development is out of line in another direction, we may conclude that he is afraid to show any signs of fear. He may be a child who feels completely unprotected by adults and tries to protect himself by avoiding feelings. Perhaps any show of emotion, any tears or hanging back are so frowned upon in his home that, to him, the greatest of all dangers appears to be displaying fear.

Such children may be headed for trouble and may need, in addition to more affection and understanding from their parents, the help of a child-guidance clinic or family counseling before they can deal with their anxieties in a more rational or constructive manner.

Whereas intense fear may produce panic or paralysis, a moderate degree of fear, when a person of any age is in real danger, heightens certain bodily processes. This, in turn, as adrenalin is poured into the bloodstream, speeds up the pulse rate, quickens responses, and adds strength and stamina. The surplus energy that often comes to the rescue of the person in time of danger or crisis is triggered by fear. Fear is therefore a protective device in some instances.

Dr. Allan S. Berger, writing in *Young Children*, says:

Anxiety itself is necessary for survival, for it stimulates the development of ways, defenses if you will, of dealing with life's dangers, both the real ones of the outer world and the make-believe ones of our inner world. It is the flashing yellow caution light on life's interminable road. . . . Anxiety is as inevitable a part of our life as our breathing and our heartbeat. Anxiety may be thought of as nature's stimulus to protect oneself.

Dr. Berger goes on to compare anxiety to the tears that form in the eyes and are often a protection to vision, although a great flow of tears interferes with seeing clearly. "What counts with anxiety," he emphasizes, "is how much of it there is and what we do with it."

Outer Pressures: Source of Some Fears

In the three-through-five age span, the children, more on their own, inevitably encounter some threatening experiences. At the age of three, in many neighborhoods, and surely at four or five, a youngster is out on the sidewalk, in somebody's yard, or at the local playground, playing with other children. Often, he will have no more supervision than that afforded by the presence of an older brother or sister engrossed in his or her own play, or an occasional checking-up-on from a mother.

Being persecuted by another child who is a bully, being chased by a frolicsome pup, or seeing a passerby whose clothes, gait, or general appearance are odd, may all seem to constitute danger to a three- or four-year-old and cause anxiety. He has not had sufficient experience to distinguish what might be unpleasant but temporary from what will plague him forever. What is merely unfamiliar gets mixed up with what is threatening.

Today, when witnessing automobile accidents can scarcely be escaped, when many children are exposed to scenes of brutality, and when television brings violence into everyone's living room, children may be anxious because of what they have seen around them. The feeling, "I may be the next one to be smashed up in a car crash" (or beaten, or even shot) is not utterly without basis.

Going to nursery school at four and kindergarten at five means separation from Mother. That, too, may be a source of anxiety. How will he get home again? What if the bus driver or the car-pool mother can't find his house? Will his mother be there when he arrives home? Inexperience and lack of understanding lead to many such painful anxieties.

Misunderstanding May Engender Fear

Coupled with more exposure to the world beyond his own home is the preschooler's active imagination. He is capable of thinking up more possibilities to worry about than he could have concocted earlier.

The four- and five-year-old listens to adult conversation and, instead of letting it flow over his head, tries to make some sense out of it. When Terry heard a visiting uncle say to her father, "So I thought it was time to nail this big shot down and make him talk turkey," she had a mental picture of that uncle nailing someone (a dangerous enemy?) to the floor and forcing him to make noises like a turkey gobbler. A pretty scary world if one's favorite uncle treats people that way!

Adults look like giants to the three- or four-year-old. He often feels frustrated and helpless because he cannot cope with doors or water faucets, steps or spoons scaled for hands that are far larger, or arms and legs that are far longer than his. When help is not forthcoming, anxiety may wash over him.

When Fears Are Generated from Within

Small children cannot always separate what has actually happened, or might happen, from their own fantasies. To a four-year-old, the witch she believes is under her bed is frighteningly real.

Along with this confounding of fact and fancy goes an exaggerated and totally unreal estimate of his own power on the part of the young child. When he gets angry, he feels that his anger is so strong that it might blow up the whole house, or destroy grown-ups.

Related to this is his mistaken notion about the potency of his wishes. A preschooler is often anxious because he has thought about doing "something bad." His parents might stop loving him and taking care of him if they knew how "bad" he was! Wishing the new baby sister would be collected with the rest of the household garbage, or that an irritable and stern visiting grandfather would go back home, seems as wicked as taking action on the wish. Then if the baby becomes mildly ill or grandfather has a fall, the hapless youngster believes his evil wishes caused the misfortune. He worries about what appears to him to be his own power for evil and about the punishment that may descend on him as a result. This point was discussed in detail in the previous chapter.

"Will I Still Be Me?"

Three-year-olds and even five-year-olds have a rather shaky sense of self. The conviction that they are separate, intact beings is still not well established. Here is another important source of anxiety that comes from within. Small children frequently are afraid they may lose a part of their bodies. Something might fall off or they might be injured. Sometimes they hint at these concerns, and sometimes they talk about them openly. Some youngsters may never display any such anxiety because they experience it only mildly or because it is thoroughly repressed from the conscious part of their personalities.

The sight of a maimed or crippled person may bring out questions: "What happened to him?" "Will that happen to me?" Perhaps no open questions are asked, but concerns may be triggered. In small boys, anxiety about bodily injury may center about the loss of their sex organ. This is discussed in Chapter 5. However, fears of losing a part of oneself are not confined to boys, or to sexual worries.

Usually this particular anxiety disappears about the time a child loses his first baby tooth. That loss demonstrates vividly that one may lose something valuable, yet not be damaged. One is still the same self. This connection between shedding a tooth and ceasing to be concerned about remaining "in one piece" was suggested by the late Dr. Harvey A. Lewis.

The Dark Is an Unknown Quantity

One of the common fears small children usually do not hesitate to show openly is their uncertainty about what the dark may hold. This fear has a number of components. Underlying it is more than merely the confusion resulting from not being able to see what is around them.

Darkness usually means the approach of bedtime, and bedtime for most children means being separated from older members of the family, who go on having a good time (or so it seems to the youngster).

Whether small children fear darkness because it brings separation and an increased sense of helplessness, or whether they fear separation because it often occurs, with its attendant loneliness, when darkness falls is a moot question. Both fears probably reinforce each other. A three- or four-year-old may find it easier to talk about the "awful monsters who come after me in the dark" than about those vague feelings of loneliness and being deserted that descend on him.

A further unpleasant aspect of lying in bed in total darkness is that all his misdeeds of the day and the reprimands that followed arise to haunt him.

Fears by Association

Utterly illogical fear may come about through the association of ideas. A three-year-old had been subjected in the course of a few weeks to a number of elderly female sitters with whom she did not enjoy staying. After that, she shrank back and often wept whenever an older woman came to her parents' home, assuming the person would be a sitter. Since her grandmother was visiting at the time, a number of elderly strangers were showing up, each of whom aroused anxiety in the small girl.

A parent who is apprehensive about his small son's or daughter's health, or about the youngster's ability to handle many everyday situations, may find his young children becoming "worry-warts."

"Gladys has inherited her mother's timidity. Her mother has always been afraid of everything. My wife, Gladys' grandmother, was always the same way. Being afraid seems to run in my wife's family," says Gladys' grandfather, who has no patience with fears of any kind.

Gladys has not *inherited* her anxious nature, but she has caught it from the way she has seen her mother respond to situations. Adults who expect the worst and are overprotective of their children convey the feeling that danger may be lurking everywhere.

Some Youngsters Are Anxiety-prone

A final, and to adults most puzzling, origin of fear in some preschool children is *the child's interpretation* of the way their parents treat them.

Nell was an extremely sensitive little girl. The slightest reproof or the gentlest teasing brought on a flood of tears. She was sure her parents preferred either the curly-haired baby sister or the boisterous older brother, both of whom appeared to her to be a threat to her own good standing. Nell soaked up affection and praise like a sponge. Nell was full of fears, chief among them that she was not pleasing her parents.

"You'd think we beat her, the way she acts if anybody corrects her the slightest bit," her father often said.

Nell was unusually susceptible to having her feelings hurt and, as a result, becoming anxious. Children of this sort are a specially demanding challenge for parents.

Fortunately, no child suffers from all these causes

of fear, nor are all his fears present all the time. On some days or in some seasons, for reasons we cannot always fathom—perhaps because of tensions within himself or in his surroundings—a youngster may be especially prone to fear. Again, for weeks or months on end, probably because conditions are favorable, manifestations of anxiety may be slight.

Built-in Devices for Defense Against Fear

In addition to the automatic physiological response to a fearsome situation, described earlier, human beings have certain mental mechanisms with which they often defend themselves against fear and make anxiety bearable. Again, no child probably employs all these devices. Some boys and girls may seem to go along without using any. Piglet, the Very Small Animal in A. A. Milne's stories about Christopher Robin and his imaginary friends, is a vehicle onto which Christopher projects his own fears. Piglet invests most of his time and energy in fussing over what might be going to happen. Since Piglet turns to Christopher for comfort, the little boy is reassuring himself when he tells Piglet that everything will be all right or laughs at his small friend's troubles.

Defending himself from fear by insisting that someone else is afraid and in need of reassurance, even though that "someone else" is an imaginary creature, is a useful device for a small child.

Denying Fear May Be a Defense Against It

An emotion that makes one too uncomfortable may be denied. Denial is somewhat different from projecting, or asserting that someone else is suffering from your fear. A five-year-old to whom the annual Fourth of July fireworks in the neighborhood park were a torment, not a treat, declared emphatically, "I'm not afraid of fireworks. I just don't like them one bit." Here was a neat bit of face-saving quite permissible in a five-year-old.

Imaginary companions, human or animal, may help a child handle his fears in several ways. In *The Magic Years*, Selma Fraiberg explains how Jan, a three-and-a-half-year-old, came to terms with her fear of animals "who could bite and might even eat a little girl up," through the invention of Laughing Tiger, an imaginary beast who came to live at her house:

> There is one place where you can meet a ferocious beast on your own terms and leave victorious. That place is the imagination. It is a matter of individual taste whether the beast should be slain, maimed, banished or reformed. Jan chose reform as her approach to the problem of ferocious animals. . . . All the dangerous attributes of tigers underwent a transformation in this new creature. This tiger doesn't bare his teeth in a savage snarl. . . . *He* is the one who is scared. . . . We suspect a parallel development here. The transformation of a tiger into an obedient and quiescent beast is probably a caricature of the civilizing process which the little girl is undergoing. . . . Jan's imaginary tiger gives her a kind of control over a danger which earlier had left her helpless and anxious.

That danger was her own impulse to be wilder or more

violent than she felt it was safe to be.

Laughing Tiger was also useful in helping Jan get over her fear of animals, Mrs. Fraiberg tells us, since he vanished at about the same time her terror of large beasts disappeared.

We are all familiar with one of the most useful means that children use to recover from a fear-inspiring incident. A youngster who has been hospitalized, lived through a hurricane, become separated from a parent in a crowd, or even had an exciting but confusing experience such as being taken to a three-ring circus, will reenact it in his play for days or perhaps weeks. As he plays it out, he gets control of it, often through playing the part of the controlling figures. It becomes more manageable, and therefore less threatening.

Being in Control Eases Fear

Rearranging a situation, figuratively or literally, so that it is no longer alarming but something of one's own creation is another constructive solution for a frightened child. Lois B. Murphy, in *The Widening World of Childhood*, tells how one small boy, Martin, dealt with his sense of being overwhelmed at a children's party. Martin became absorbed in building high, narrow structures out of big cardboard bricks. He paid no attention to the other children or the people coming into the room. In doing so, he was proving to himself that his building, not the party, was the important matter for him. He had altered the situation to suit his own taste by isolating himself from it, so that the party as such hardly existed for him.

Four-year-old Delia "rearranged a situation" when

she moved, with her parents and her younger sister, to a new home in another city. Her parents had rented a furnished apartment belonging to a woman who also had two small daughters, so Delia walked into a room equipped for girls her own age. Still, she was uneasy and anxious. She took one look around. Then she began tugging at the two small chairs and the low table. She pushed and tugged until chairs and table were where she wanted them. She changed the position of the two mats on the floor.

"Now," she declared to her admiring younger sister, "it's how we like it best, isn't it?"

Marshaling One's Forces

Another device for coping with anxiety described in Dr. Murphy's book is "surveying the situation." Another boy, at the party referred to earlier, came in, stood with his hands in his pockets, and looked over the scene. "This surveying," says Dr. Murphy, "often implies 'defining a safe area,' since in order to survey a situation one must first have secured an observation point."

Mr. Brand, whose five-year-old son was addicted to "defining a safe area" when he was in a situation threatening to him, felt the boy was "hanging back and acting like a baby." Mr. Brand refused to understand that the boy, by getting his bearings when he was under stress, was frequently able to turn a threat into a challenge, but a challenge cut down to a size he could handle. By pushing the boy, the father too often interfered with his son's style of dealing with fear, and by disapproving of it, deprived the little boy of an important, healthy prop.

The Unfamiliar Is Alarming

Protecting oneself against anxiety by being sure everything is in its accustomed place, that no detail of one's surroundings is altered, is a device that is useful in moderation. For a two- or two-and-a-half-year-old, insisting on the precise repetition of routines is quite natural. A five-year-old can be expected to be more flexible. Breakfast cereal served in a different bowl, or the announcement that a favorite blanket will be unavailable for a night because it is being washed, is less devastating at five than at two. Even in an emotionally healthy five-year-old, however, there may still be some protest.

The necessity for keeping objects in the same place and events in exactly the same sequence to ward off panic is usually a sign, in children of five or older, that they are afraid that if one detail is altered the whole fabric of their lives will fall apart. Children who have been subjected to frequent upheavals in their lives, such as sudden, unpredictable, prolonged absences of a mother or father, or losing a parent and being moved from one foster home to another, may take refuge from their anxiety in elaborate rituals to be sure neither objects nor events are getting out of control.

Displacing Fear onto Another

Admitting, even to themselves, that they are sometimes afraid of an adult they love and on whom they are dependent is painful for young children. This was the case with Harry, who found his father an intimidating person, more because he was such a big man than because he ever threatened or hurt the boy. Harry, when he was three, was terrified of bears. Pictures of bears, let alone the real thing in the zoo, sent him into spells of near hysteria.

Harry had displaced his trepidation about his father onto bears, real and imaginary. That was a fear more easily borne. Like many large men, Harry's father was quite gentle in his manner, but what came on strong for Harry was his bulk.

The unwarranted fear of large animals can have such a variety of implications in the emotional economy of the young that considering it, as we have, from several points of view may be instructive.

When Attack Becomes a Defense

Children who grow up in surroundings that seem to present constant danger may come to believe that the best way to reduce the fear of attack is to become the attacker. Their suspicions that their contemporaries are about to strike out at them or snatch a toy away and their anxiety about the possible scoldings or even blows adults may deal them are usually exaggerated, if not completely false. Even when no threat exists, when they are with children or grown-ups who are obviously friendly, such youngsters are poised for an angry response. Clearly, this is among the destructive defenses.

Once more, an excellent example is to be found in Milne's *The House at Pooh Corner*, this time in the person of the bouncy animal, Tigger, who attacks without provocation. This creature arrived at the house of the amiable Pooh in the small hours of the morning. He had not been there long when he said:

"Excuse me a moment, but there's something climbing up your table," and with one loud *worraworraworra* he jumped at the end of the table-cloth, pulled it to the ground, wrapped himself up in it three times . . . and after a terrible struggle, got his head into the daylight again and said cheerfully: "Have I won?"

"That's my tablecloth," said Pooh and he began to unwind Tigger.

"I wondered what it was," said Tigger.

"It goes on the table and you put things on it."

"Then why did it try to bite me when I wasn't looking?"

"I don't *think* it did," said Pooh.

"It tried," said Tigger, "but I was too quick for it."

Frequently, children who have not had loving parents, who have not known the security of consistent treatment in a stable home, express their mistrust of their surroundings by becoming quick to strike out. Such children, five or ten years later, are the ones described as "hard to reach." They have built a wall of angry pugnaciousness around themselves as protection from an all-consuming fear.

Looking for Reassurance

A defense against fear resorted to by almost every child who has a kindly adult available is to seek reassurance frequently and emphatically. Nina, when she was three, was afraid of the whirring vacuum cleaner, the whining of a siren, the buzzing of a telephone left off its hook. When she heard such noises she ran to her mother and insisted on being held. For an hour or more afterward she would follow her mother around, clinging to her and demanding, "Noise gone? More noise coming?"

Like many of the means children employ to come to terms with fear and anxiety, this one is useful in moderation. Only when a youngster tries to solve his problems by rigidly overdoing some defense to the exclusion of any other kind of behavior do we need to feel the situation is a potentially serious one. We may expect to have three-, four-, and five-year-olds try out inappropriate means of dealing with fears.

We cannot hope to eradicate the fears of the preschool period, but we can often help children manage them. A first step in this direction is to set an example of buoyancy, hopefulness, and a reasonable degree of control. In wartime, in disasters such as floods or earthquakes, as well as in less cataclysmic domestic crises, children with adults who do not panic tend to be less disturbed. That does not mean that parents need always suppress their own doubts and difficulties. But if a mother and father can stay calm when, for example, on a family automobile trip Father takes the wrong road and they are momentarily "lost," or when one parent is unaccountably late in arriving home, the children are less apt to develop the habit of being anxious. If every mishap is the signal for extreme worry and dire forebodings, let alone recriminations, a child naturally comes to believe that is the way to meet uncertainty or mishaps.

Fortunately, today we are not so likely to insist that a young child, particularly a boy, keep "a stiff upper lip" when he is frightened. In many families but, alas, not all, small boys are permitted to own up to being afraid at times without being shamed, ridiculed, or made to feel unworthy. We know now that feelings are more easily dealt with if they are out in the open. To add disgrace for betraying certain feelings to the burden of being anxious only compounds a child's troubles.

Reassurance in words is not guaranteed to alleviate fears, but it often helps. "We will take good care of you." "We'll all be (or "We all are) together." "I know this seems sort of scary, but Daddy is right here with you." "When I was as big as you are now, I was afraid sometimes, too, but it got better. After a while you won't feel so frightened." Phrases like these can give more support, as a rule, than denying that any cause for fear exists. "There's nothing to be scared of," makes a youngster feel he is foolish as well as anxious.

When a child has lived through an alarming incident such as being hurt or seeing someone badly injured, being separated from his parents in a crowd, or being bullied by a bigger child, he can be allowed to talk about it. The incident need not become the central fact in life, nor should he be encouraged to rehearse it for everyone he meets. Yet he will probably recover more readily if he can ask questions, receive reassurance, and not feel the subject is taboo within the family.

Introducing New Situations Gradually

The unknown usually arouses some measure of anxiety. A sensible amount of preparation when a child must face a strange set of circumstances assists him in coping more effectively.

For example, a preparatory visit to the dentist when an older brother or sister or a parent is the patient, talking over what the dentist will do and will not do, as well as some explanation of why going to the dentist is necessary, may reduce anxiety about the first dental examination.

Preparation for an event that might be intimidating can frequently take the form of playing out with one's youngster the part he and others will take in the untried situation. This kind of playacting is described in detail in Chapter 9.

Unfamiliar experiences in small doses, when that is possible, often prevent the unknown from being so taxing that the boy or girl ends up exhausted and therefore more prone to be anxious.

Reexposure Tends to Make Matters Worse

Philip, when he was three, was afraid of the merry-go-round on the playground where he spent some time each day, in good weather, with his mother. She felt that Philip found more than enough to do without being forced to go on the merry-go-round. His father believed that avoiding a showdown over merry-go-rounds was coddling the boy. He coerced Philip into getting on the merry-go-round. The boy fell off—his father said "on purpose." Although he was not badly hurt, his prejudice against this whirling device was reinforced. The next day his father insisted he must go back and try again, or "He'll be afraid the rest of his life."

The second attempt left Phil in a state bordering on panic. Not only, thereafter, was he more afraid than ever of rapidly revolving, dizzying machines, even revolving doors, but he was also afraid to go to the playground. And *that* created an impasse for his mother, as it was his main contact with other children and the neighborhood's best resource for outdoor play.

Action Brings Courage

Giving children something to do to meet a potential danger tends to reduce their sense of helplessness. A family who lived in an area where tornado warnings were frequent developed a useful plan. When warnings on radio or TV indicated that their own neighborhood might be in the direct path of a storm, each one, including the four-year-old, undertook certain assigned duties. As a result both of taking action and of feeling "I know what to do," anxiety was diminished.

Another family effectively reduced the children's fears of the house burning down, the electric power going off, and other remote, but possible, contingencies that the children had heard about or seen on television by talking over what each one was to do in case any such emergency arose. The mother and father stressed to the children the protection the community provided and how to summon help or use the materials and resources on hand. The emphasis on constructive action, the fact that "Something can be done about it if . . . ," rather than "How awful it would be if . . . ," helped the children remain calmer when emergencies did arise and less anxious about dangers in general.

In a one-parent family, if no relatives live nearby,

both the children and the parent may feel especially vulnerable. "What would we do if some night you didn't come home from work?" Lois, aged four, often demanded of her mother. Her mother finally decided to tell her that if anything like that ever happened, and it was unlikely that it would, and if the woman who looked after Lois could not stay on with her, Lois should go to their friends the Thompsons, who lived downstairs. Lois' mother was careful to tell Mrs. Thompson what she had told Lois. The mother also made sure that Lois knew the full name and address of her grandparents, who lived in a nearby city, and that the Thompsons also had that information and the telephone number of the firm where Lois' mother worked. These arrangements were a great relief to this little girl.

Night Terrors

During the preschool years many children go through a period when they wake up screaming because of a bad dream. Even if they don't cry out, they may be so anxious that they go into their parents' bedroom and beg to be taken into the parents' bed. Here firmness is needed from mothers and fathers. "Children sleep in their own beds, not with grown-ups," is a doctrine that may need to be repeated again and again. A frightened child needs to be comforted and taken back to his own bed. Difficult as it is to get up, patiently return the child to bed, and sit beside him until he is quiet or has fallen asleep, the unfortunate long-term results and complications that parents avoid by not letting a small son or daughter share their bed even in a one-parent family, "just this once," are worth the effort.

Some parents have tried to eradicate fear of the dark and night terrors by taking the small child by the hand as darkness falls and sitting with him in the shadows. They have talked about how the furniture, the doors and windows change their appearance, but nothing is in the room that isn't present when it is well lighted. Making a game of going into a darkened room, holding the youngster's hand, and "exploring"— trying to recognize familiar objects by touching them— is another device that has been tried. These techniques may reduce the fears of some children and are surely worth a trial, but night terrors come, not so much from the absence of light, as from within the child's own, often unconscious, feelings. Rational explanations do not drive out irrational fears. (Chapter 7 discusses this question further.)

If we suspect that our three- or four- or five-year-old awakens during the night "just to get attention," we might try giving him more pleasant, affectionate attention during the day. Everything that we can do to build up his conviction that we approve of him will tend to make him less prone to unwarranted anxieties and will probably help him more than logical explanations or experiments with light, shadows, and darkness.

Leaving doors open or nightlights burning may bring an anxious child comfort, and are not to be considered appeasement or coddling. They will not ruin his independence, but may strengthen it. A favorite blanket or a cuddly stuffed animal may also decrease his loneliness and fears. If the demand for stuffed animals gets so voracious that a youngster wants all seven of his favorites each night, we may need to specify that one or two are sufficient.

Unfortunately, there is no neat formula for banishing nighttime fears. A parent, weary from sitting up during the night with a panicky child, can only be assured that groundless anxieties tend to diminish as a youngster's understanding of what is real and what is "pretend" becomes clearer. As he is better able to distinguish between events that are beyond his control and those for which he is held responsible, his fears will usually become less intense. Experiences that tell him that the unfamiliar may be pleasant and that the new is not necessarily painful also decrease overall apprehension. We can foster such maturity, but we cannot expect it to be full-blown in the years before six.

9

Encouraging Independence

G ROWTH IN INDEPENDENCE in preschoolers comes in
two flavors. The "sweet" kind, for both parents
and children, includes such practical progress as dressing without assistance, being out-of-doors without direct
supervision, fetching and carrying in the house, and
running errands or taking a message to a neighbor. Parents usually welcome and make an effort to provide
practice in these forms of independence.

A youngster's ability to accept brief separations
from his parents with equanimity; to solve problems
that arise in his play without more than a hint from an
adult; to figure out the relationship between events,
occasionally; and to brush off, rather than seek, hugs,
kisses, and cuddling are among the forms of independence we might call "semisweet" or "bittersweet."
Mothers and fathers may find it more difficult to create
opportunities for the children to practice this variety.

They may also respond with less obvious enthusiasm to their son's or daughter's self-reliance in thinking and feeling. Then, the youngsters, since they seem to be receiving less approval, tend to get less satisfaction from the "semisweet" behavior. The two flavors come in a double package. Both are vital in a child's total development. Each is closely tied to the other.

As a boy or girl moves toward more independent behavior of all kinds, he or she changes in ways that bring mixed emotions to both generations. Pride in a child's advance is often laced with parental regret when, for instance, a five-year-old shows signs of preferring the company of a playmate to that of his parents or his grandparents. Or when, at four and a half or five and a half, he counters adults' rather flimsy reasons for prohibiting some scheme of his own with arguments that make fairly good sense. If his proposals are couched in language suggesting that the grown-ups are not quite as bright as they might be, independent thinking will hardly be regarded as an asset by those grown-ups.

"It is *too* warm enough to take off my sweater. Don't you think I know when I'm cold or not? You ought to have your head examined." Such statements may show a burgeoning capacity to make judgments, for all their lack of diplomacy.

Our youngster also experiences a two-way pull about assuming independent behavior. Healthy children want to grow up, yet when things go wrong—when they are tired, or ill, or distressed—they will slide back to wanting more help, more affection, and more reassurance. As a result of both our conflicting feelings and his own, a child will probably acquire self-reliance in a "two steps forward, one step backward" fashion. Letting go of babyish behavior, even in small ways, carries a threat for him of losing us completely.

Independence Has Deep Roots

Many of the characteristics that are strands in a well-knit personality are components of self-sufficiency. Confidence in oneself and faith in the predictability of one's surroundings, a sense of being a separate individual who can make good things happen, a degree of resiliency and resourcefulness, as well as courage and imagination, underlie self-reliance.

Independence has its beginnings long before the age of three (as Sara Gilbert explains in her book *Three Years to Grow*). In the strictest sense, it starts when a baby takes his first breath. Developing initiative, trying out his powers to explore and experiment has been labeled by Erik Erikson as a central need for the child in the years from three through five. Such initiative forms the basis of independent action, though it is often of the "semisweet" brand. No student of the preschool years, including Erikson, would attempt to sum up the ramifications of development of this period in one neat phrase. Too much is going on, especially in the fluctuations between "I can do it," and "I can't do it. I don't know how." (The question of initiative is also discussed in Chapters 1 and 11 of this volume.)

Home Atmosphere Affects Independence

Families communicate to their young, without putting anything into words, what degree of self-determination and how wide a choice are permitted by their own ethnic or religious traditions, the customs of the neighborhood, and their individual aspirations and fears. Parents who see life as offering a number of options in such matters as where one lives, how one spends one's leisure time, and what kind of work one does tend to convey to their children a feeling of flexibility and range in the possibilities open to them. Their youngsters are allowed the pleasure of planning their lives in small ways. "Shall we go to the zoo or do you want to go to the playground next Sunday?" Here is a simple choice, but it offers a degree of flexibility and independence. Opportunities to make selections imply that more than one way can be good. They engender the feeling in the child that decision-making and planning are worth some mental effort because they can lead to getting what he wants.

Contrast this with the feeling that a child absorbs in a home where the parental mood varies between vague uneasiness and seething fury because, "*They* won't let us do what we want to anyway"; "*They* will be down on our necks if we want to try anything." The unspecified "they" might be dominating parents, demanding, among other forms of deference, that married sons and daughters and their offspring assemble weekly and meekly for a "family night" whose warmth has cooled and whose usefulness has been outgrown. Or the oft-invoked and forbidding "they" might be a landlord, employer, or some group who are seen as being, or actually are, an acute menace. In such a family, children are not encouraged to make thoughtful plans or see independent thinking or acting as a means of attaining one's ends. Parents sunk in futility convey the message "What's the use?" to even the smallest children.

In discussing the significance to preschoolers of opportunities for independent thinking, Robert Hess and Virginia Shipman report, as a result of their research:

Possibilities for alternative ways of action and thought encourage children to consider [those] alternatives, to select, to develop criteria for choice and to learn the basic elements of decision-making and anticipating the future consequences of present action.

Decision-making: Ages Three Through Five

Appropriate opportunities to make choices in everyday living enhance young children's feeling that they have a part in making good things happen through effort and foresight. One point to remember is that when we say, "It's up to you. You decide which you want," we need to offer alternatives among which a child may safely and realistically make a selection. Many decisions are beyond a child's capacity to make, and being told they are his to make puts a frightening and false burden on him. We don't, for instance, allow him to choose whether or not to eat breakfast. But whether breakfast should begin with fruit or cereal, or even include a cheese sandwich, might well be a matter of individual taste, provided a mother, father, or older brother or sister in charge of preparing breakfast has time to cater to a four-year-old's preference.

If a child has to take what comes at family meals,

snack time might give scope to his selective powers. Again, the choice would need to be confined to available, sensible items. "Jelly sandwich? Apple? Raisins?" would make more sense than "What do you want for a snack?" The latter might lead to a demand for forbidden foods or ones not on hand.

A youngster can be allowed to choose, within reason, which of his clothes he will wear. If an unharmonious combination of colors seems to be his heart's desire, what's so terrible about that? But if it is a question of shorts versus slacks in frigid weather, or if wearing new shoes when playing in the mud is on the agenda, then parental wisdom needs to take precedence.

If finding playmates is not a spontaneous matter and involves some arranging by a mother, a child's own choice deserves to be listened to. Of course, his choice may not coincide with his parents', but he may have sounder reasons for it than are immediately apparent.

Family Relationships and Independence

Self-reliance is influenced, too, by the tone of the interaction between a child and his parents. One study has shown that in a home where relationships are warm, where mothers and fathers say "Yes" whenever they reasonably can rather than saying "No" as a matter of course to requests, questioning, or spontaneity of any kind, the child tends to show more independence, or "ease in assuming responsibility for his own behavior." Even when parents were warm and loving, but rules were numerous and restrictive, the children did not easily become "self-starters" who could take responsibility for themselves, the study showed.

Backsliding May Precede Advancement

Independence, then, has its roots both in the child's own drive to be an individual and exercise initiative and in the way the family and the neighborhood view attempts to be innovative.

Recognizing the conflicting feelings both parents and children have about advances in self-reliance, we can see why a five-year-old or three-year-old cannot do today what he did with ease yesterday.

How can we give youngsters the feeling that though we welcome their increasing self-sufficiency, we still love and accept them when they need more help than usual, but that we will protect them from too much backsliding by setting limits below which regression shall not go?

Mr. and Mrs. Rand handled Chuck's frequent returns to helplessness in a more effective manner than did a sister and brother-in-law who also had a four-year-old. When Chuck insisted he could not get his socks on, or that he had "forgotten" how to put knives and forks on the supper table, or balked at assuming some small responsibility that usually gave him satisfaction, his mother would try encouragement first. If that brought no results, she would say something such as, "Oh, well, I guess we all have days when we can't do our 'first best.' I'll help you with one sock, and tomorrow I know you'll be able to put both on by yourself."

If Chuck's father was around when one of the "I can't do it" moods hit the little boy, he would take the line, "You're teasing me! I'll bet you can do it before I look at you again." If that approach was ineffective, he might say, "O.K. Let's do it together *this time.*" Letting Chuck know he was expected to resume his usual degree of independence in time was a face-saving device for the boy and also put a floor under his return to babyishness.

Sometimes the fluctuation in self-sufficiency took other forms. Chuck might hold tightly to his mother's hand while they were at the supermarket or ask to ride in the cart in which she put her purchases, both of which were customs he had long ago relinquished. Sometimes his temporarily diminished independence took the form of not wanting to leave home to play at another child's house.

Mrs. Rand's sister-in-law held the view that any outpost in independence once won must be maintained or the entire struggle for self-reliance would be lost. When her son had one of those days when he seemed more like two and a half than four and a half, she would say, "Aren't you ashamed of yourself, a big boy like you, not wanting to . . ." etc., etc. By the end of her tirade he *was* ashamed. He was also afraid his un-expendable mother would abandon him as a hopeless case, although those were hardly the phrases he could have used to express his abysmal feeling of disgrace.

This boy tended to have less resilience, as a small child, and later on, than did his cousin Chuck. Although the more Spartan sister-in-law criticized Mrs. Rand's "permissiveness" as coddling and predicted dire results for Chuck, nothing of the sort occurred.

The "I Can Do It" Feelings

Self-reliance may, for equally unfathomable reasons, take a sudden leap forward. Each of us has occasionally arisen on a bright morning feeling equal to anything, or almost anything. That day we breeze through tasks, amazed at how much we accomplish with so little effort.

Small children are subject to the same heightened abilities from time to time. Then, independent behavior gets a boost. Each time this occurs and a youngster discovers that he really can enjoy putting his outdoor boots on by himself, carrying a pitcher of milk from the refrigerator to the table without spilling it, or whatever may be the fresh achievement, he gains an inch more self-reliance, a bit more of the feeling, "I can do it myself."

In discussing the "I can do it" feelings in *The Widening World of Childhood*, a study of how children cope with their environment, Lois B. Murphy says:

> Each experience of mastery is not only a momentary conquest, but a promise of more to come, a reassurance of the capacity to grow up. The sense of mastery is also closely related to a sense of worth, importance and ability to gain respect from others and maintain one's own self-respect. . . . we may infer that mastery and coping ability are closely involved with the sense of identity. Through his coping experiences the child discovers and measures himself, and develops his own perception of who and what he is and, in time, may become.

These components of the "I can do it" feelings serve to undergird independence and prevent momentary lapses in self-reliance from becoming complete collapse. The sudden and often unaccountable spurts in "I can do it" behavior are like money in the savings bank. This surplus confidence, like money earning interest, accumulates and can be drawn on in the event of an emotional "rainy day," when self-doubt and discouragement need a corrective.

Here, again, we see the importance of the child's own picture of himself as "the kind who can do it," which he derives from what his parents say and the way they treat him. The stronger his sense that his parents approve of him and that "he is all right as he is," the more readily will he achieve a self-sufficiency appropriate to his age.

Eve, a five-year-old who was small for her age, had frequently been praised for being independent in a family in which that trait was highly valued. Eve was asked by a visiting aunt to go upstairs to the aunt's bedroom, find a package, and return with it to the backyard where the family was assembled. Her aunt explained exactly where it was and then said, somewhat condescendingly, "Do you think you can do that, Evie?"

"Oh, yes, I can, Aunt Kate. I'm *very* independent, even though I'm not exactly a great, big giant of a girl."

Eve's firm conviction that her small size was no barrier to her being competent did credit to the feelings her parents had instilled.

Managing Buttons and Bows

The "I can do it" feelings find expression in a pride in mastering dressing and undressing, washing, bathing, taking responsibility for toileting, and helping around the house. Mothers and fathers can facilitate the accomplishment of such tasks by providing clothing and equipment that the threes, fours, and fives can handle.

Children's clothes today can be blessedly simple to get into and out of, and getting out of them is usually the skill acquired first. Nobody has raised a statue to the inventor of the zipper and inscribed it, "Benefactor of Children," but he merits such recognition!

Whenever possible, outdoor clothing for children should have good-sized zippers that do not present a problem to muscles not yet perfectly coordinated. The easiest way for a child to put on a sweater, jacket, or any garment opening down the front is to spread it out on the floor with the open side uppermost. The youngster stands in back of the top of the garment, leans over, and puts his arms through the sleeves. Then he can swing it over his head, straighten up, and to his delight, he has put it on by himself. A three-year-old can easily do this and also learn to spread his garment out quite easily.

Laying pants out on the floor makes it easy for the youngster to wriggle into them. Clothing that is big enough to get into and out of easily may be less trim than tight-fitting slacks and "T" shirts or turtleneck sweaters with small openings at the neck; but if our goal is an independent, comfortably dressed boy or girl rather than a fashion plate, we should see that clothes fit loosely without being so large that they are droopy.

In a climate that makes snow boots and mittens a necessity, the boots should be big enough to get into readily. The old-fashioned device of sewing mittens to each end of a tape that goes around the back of the neck and through the sleeves of a coat cuts down on wasted time and temper expended in searching for a lost mitten.

One skill in dressing that usually is not acquired until around the age of six is the tying of shoelaces into firm knotted bows.

What Some Mothers Have Done

Experienced mothers have their own bits of wisdom on increasing proficiency in the dressing, washing, and bathing department. Some say that their three- and four-year-olds can manage to get into their clothes in the morning if they are allowed to dress in the kitchen where their mothers are preparing breakfast. One mother relates:

We have a two-story house. If I had insisted that Hank dress himself before he came downstairs, he'd have been left on the second floor alone, because his father is at breakfast by the time I get Hank up, and I'm giving the baby her cereal. My mother considers letting a child dress in the kitchen and trail around with one sock in his hand while he's drinking his orange juice "bad training," but it works. Hank does get dressed, and pretty well for a three-and-a-half-year-old.

Another mother, who has four children, says that the two older ones are each assigned a younger brother or sister whose dressing, toothbrushing, and hand and face washing he supervises in the morning. That means that the supervisors of the three- and four-and-a-half-year-old are themselves barely six and seven, but everybody grows in independence in this arrangement. "The two older ones actually expect more from the younger ones than I would, and they get better results, too," this mother reports.

For some four- and five-year-olds, the only necessary cues for dressing are to have clothes selected and laid out the night before. Having underwear, pants, shirt, and socks out in plain sight avoids demands for help on the grounds that "I can't find it."

Is Cleanliness Next to Impossible?

Another mother's recipe for independent grooming is a sturdy footstool or wooden box or step just high enough for the boy or girl to reach the faucets in the washbasin and the supplies he needs. "Once the youngsters can understand how to mix the hot water with the cold so they aren't half scalded, they can manage to get themselves reasonably clean. What we lose in spic-and-span grooming, we make up for in pride in being on one's own," the father in this family says.

One young child brought up on this principle expressed his feelings about it interestingly. He had been sent to clean up before supper when his parents had a guest. He reappeared so quickly that he could hardly have done a thorough job. His mother looked at his still-grimy hands, but said nothing. When she was tucking him in bed that evening, her son said to her, "I'm glad you didn't send me back to wash over again. I'd have been embarrassed."

His mother told him she understood that, and that next time he would, she was sure, do better. Be it said, he did.

At bathtime, soaping knees and elbows and scrubbing arms and legs with a soft brush are tasks after a preschooler's own heart. The question is more often how to get him out of the tub than to interest him in washing. For the three-year-old, and even the four-year-old, supervision on a safety basis is still wise. The threes can all too easily become frisky, slip, and have a serious accident if left alone for long.

Other Ways to Help

Independence is also fostered, some parents attest, by having low hooks within easy reach in the bathroom on which the children can hang towels and/or nightclothes. Hooks they can reach in closets and entryways point up the lesson that clothes are hung up. "My very own place" to put clothes and other possessions means a great deal to a small child.

One father made a set of cubbyholes to stand near the back door, so that outdoor boots could be stashed away and found again without appealing to the adults for help.

By age three, children have usually learned to go to the toilet alone, but they may still require reminders before leaving the house or when they are absorbed in play. Threes and fours may still need assistance in wiping themselves clean after a bowel movement, but the fives can usually take care of themselves. An increasing desire for privacy in the bathroom, if it is respected, also adds to independence.

Some three-year-olds go through the night without being taken to the toilet; others will wake and ask to go to the bathroom. Picking up a soundly sleeping youngster, placing him on the toilet, and encouraging him to urinate while he is only half awake does not usually contribute to his taking responsibility for staying dry through the night. Parents may hesitate to put an end to that practice, lest he either wet his bed or awaken his parents later in the night. Experimenting with not waking the youngster sometimes proves he no longer needs the prop of nighttime toileting.

Many four- and five-year-olds who still need to get up during the night can take care of their own needs if they are given a flashlight or if their route to the bathroom is lighted with the small bulbs that fit into floor sockets and cast a sufficient glow to dispel complete darkness.

Mealtime independence usually makes strides during these years. From clutching a small fork or spoon at three, a youngster progresses to using both fork and spoon quite neatly, even helping himself to vegetables or potatoes from a serving dish, if it is held for him. Spreading peanut butter or jelly with a knife is within the powers of many fives. Judgment about what size portions to take, or to request, is still lacking.

Three-year-olds may dawdle over a meal, but five-year-olds infrequently need to be told to finish up. The pace may still be slow, especially if they are engaged in conversation, but they are usually steady eaters. Cutting their meat, or even cutting something as soft as a pancake or a waffle, helping themselves to gravy or a sauce, unless it can be poured from a pitcher, may still be beyond them. "Finger foods," such as raw carrot, celery, or zucchini sticks, hard-cooked egg wedges, and sandwiches make independent eating easier.

Preschoolers enjoy "clearing" and by the age of four are good at taking plates or glasses, one at a time, from kitchen table to sink, or from the family's dining area to the kitchen. This can be a real help, but it also gives small children a legitimate reason for leaving the table and moving around between the main course and dessert when prolonged sitting still becomes tedious.

If the family has a meal at a restaurant or lunch counter, the preschoolers enjoy choosing and announcing their choice of food. (Is it ever anything except hamburger, hot dog, or the peanut-butter sandwich they would eat at home?) Independence can be as growth-promoting when it is a treat as when it is a task, and encouraging youngsters to state what they want, briefly but politely, affords them practice in making a choice and in looking after themselves.

Household Chores Come in All Sizes

One form of independence mothers and fathers would like to instill, but that the young do not always respond to, is the putting away of toys and play equipment. First aid for implementing this worthy custom is to provide a place that is accessible for storing playthings. The time-honored "toy chest," which can be anything from a fiberboard box to a sturdy wooden one, has in its favor that toys can be quickly tossed in, but playthings do get broken and unaccountably "lost" in such a receptacle. If space is available, low shelves are often the most desirable arrangement.

Picking up can be aided, too, by judicious timing. One mother recommends:

Don't wait until the kids are all tired out to tell them to put their gear away, and don't make it a grim deal. I sing something silly, like "Heigh-ho, heigh-ho, it's cleanup time, you know," and then I improvise some lines to go with the rest of the jingle, and we're on our way. I stick around to give them some hints and lend a hand from time to time. The important thing is that they learn that toys are put away and that an orderly room is pleasanter to live in than a messy one. If they've built some really terrific bridge, or what not, or have some "work in progress" they want to come back to, that we leave standing.

In another family, a different plan has been found effective. The father describes it this way:

When our three-year-old and five-and-a-half-year-old are through playing, they're tired. So before my wife or I tell them it's time to put things away, one of us sits down for a few minutes and tells them a story, or we just look at a picture book, or have a game of "hide the thimble" or "I see something blue" or another game. Then we say, "Now everybody's had a rest, you can put your stuff away." Usually—mind you, not always, because there is no magic to these things—they get the room in fairly good shape without more than one or two complaints about each other. Sometimes we put on a record or get some music on the radio to help them keep going.

Young children usually enjoy helping in other ways far more than they relish picking up in their own quarters or their assigned play space. Fours and fives can, after their own fashion, make their beds. The result may be a bit lumpy, but they get "A" for effort, and we can take the will for the deed. One small girl delighted in being "beauty operator" for her mother and taking out the rollers from her mother's hair.

Feeding the family pets is another responsibility they enjoy but need to be reminded about. The consequences of neglect are far too serious to allow a small boy or girl to have a starved turtle or even a hungry puppy on his conscience.

Drying dishes, particularly the nonbreakable ones; putting away small items that have been laundered; storing groceries brought home from the store are not beyond four- and five-year-old competence. Fetching the morning newspaper, bringing in supplies the milk-man has left at the door, emptying wastebaskets are traditionally the jobs of the youngest. Some fives can water house plants if they are given a small pitcher for the water. Table-setting is not beyond the scope of the three-year-old. A toy floor mop and broom may make it possible for four- and five-year-olds to "help" with floor care, but their zeal flags quickly. They are interested only in manipulating the broom or mop for a minute or two rather than in getting any given floor space clean. The same principle applies to dusting low tables or shelves that they can negotiate but usually won't stay with long enough to be useful.

Other Aids Toward Independence

In the cooking department, convenience foods give the smallest cooks a chance to try their hand at gelatin desserts and prepared pudding mixes. Mothers need to stand by if boiling water or scalded milk are to be handled. Muffin and cookie mixes, with a little super-vision, may turn out to be edible products that give five-year-olds a gratifying sense of competence.

"Being a messenger" made one three-and-a-half-year-old feel extremely important. Her father would ask her to find out from her mother whether he had time before supper to get the car filled with gas, or her mother would say, "Daddy was looking for the newspaper.

Here it is. Will you take it to him?" When this young messenger was a bit older, her services expanded to her parents' friends in the apartment building. "You could go downstairs and tell Mrs. Cable that you and I bought a new kind of bun at the bakery and if she'd like to come up and join us, we'll have a coffee party." Other instructions of a no more complex nature, carefully carried through, added to her feeling that she could handle a situation by herself.

Even fairly self-reliant five-year-olds may not relish being sent upstairs after dark to get Grandma's glasses for her or to find Mother's lipstick.

Carrying out household tasks, according to his own ability to persevere and to use his hands deftly, and being praised for his helpfulness, tend to reinforce a child's picture of himself as one who can achieve independence. But studies carried out at the University of Minnesota by Dale Harris and his associates showed that doing routine tasks did not carry over and enhance a real sense of responsibility during the later years of childhood and adolescence.

The World Beyond Home

Independence has so many facets that sometimes we lose sight of that useful tool for building it: being in another home for brief or more extended visits unaccompanied by a parent. Some children are fortunate in that they grow up in a friendly neighborhood and/or near relatives. Then, being in and out of other people's homes is just an agreeable part of everyday life. No planning for it is necessary. Four-year-old Jimmy feels at home in three or four households in the apartment complex where he lives. Five-year-old Shirley wanders in and out of the Schmidts' house next door to her own, and of the O'Malleys' a few houses down the block, to inquire if her contemporaries are available, and possibly settles down for a visit with Mr. O'Malley or the grandmother who shares the Schmidt home. Nobody thinks of this as "training for independence." When we contrast the lot of the child who has no opportunities, such as Jimmy and Shirley have, to be on his own away from home, informally and spontaneously, we see how much such a boy or girl is losing.

Enough self-reliance to make visits at least tolerable, and hopefully pleasant, comes with practice. Visiting is also discussed in Chapter 3.

Says the father of a rather clinging small girl:

We fed Marcia chances to be away from home in the tiniest portions. We had no relatives within a hundred miles, so Marcie missed out on that fine old custom of "spending the day with grandma," which had been a part of my childhood. You can't expect casual acquaintances to take a lot of trouble with a weepy visitor, so before we let Marcie stay somewhere without her mother or me, we made sure she knew the people and the house well, could find the bathroom, and all that sort of thing. Then, we worked up gradually to letting her stay for a meal, and finally, when she liked the idea, overnight. It was a slow business, but it worked. Before she entered first grade, Marcie had several friends with whom she liked to "sleep over." She had even spent a weekend with an aunt in another city.

Since independence feeds on itself, these gratifying experiences of Marcie's also made other steps in self-sufficiency easier.

One resourceful mother played out with her young children just what kinds of things would be likely to happen and what they might be expected to do when they went visiting or "slept over." First she would let the youngster take the part of the adult hostess or host. "What do you think Karen's mother will say to you when you get there with your suitcase?," etc. The mother would take the part of the young host or the visitor. She and her four- or five-year-old would go through playtime, mealtime, bedtime conversations, changing the roles around so that the about-to-be visitor absorbed the feeling of each role and felt more at ease about what he or she would need to do in this new situation.

The grandfather of a four-year-old who was packing up to "sleep over" at a neighbor's house looked askance at the excited preparations. "I'll bet those two monkeys stay up until after midnight and are up at the crack of dawn again. You'll have one tired and crabby boy on your hands when he comes home tomorrow. Is it worth it?"

"You may be right, Pops, but Buddy's so proud of being able to go all by himself, and it's such a big step forward for him to deal with being away from home, that a little crabbiness will be a small price to pay," Buddy's mother told her father-in-law.

Nursery School and Independence
Nursery schools as an aid to sociability were dis-

cussed in Chapter 3. Any thoughts about encouraging independence must also include the contribution a nursery school or neighborhood play group can make to a child's growth in self-reliance.

Good nursery schools offer a child-paced world in which a youngster can use initiative, follow up on ideas of his own, experiment with materials, and be independent in a setting that is at once safe, stimulating, and sociable.

Greta Mayer and Mary Hoover, in the booklet *Learning to Love and to Let Go,* say:

> It rarely makes sense to enroll a child in nursery school unless he says, after visiting it and being told what goes on there, that he wants to go. Of course it may not always work even then. . . . If you decide to send your child to nursery school, or enroll him in any formal group activity, be prepared to stick around for the first few sessions. . . . Don't feel you've made a terrible mistake if Johnny clings to you at first. . . . Also don't appear especially anxious to leave. . . . It should be made clear to him that you and his teacher expect him to manage in time to get along without his mother. Be sure that the clinging is all on his part, not yours. Don't hover over him or try to tell him what to do. . . . If you can make your child feel that your love for him includes confidence in his ability to adjust to this new experience, you strengthen his wish to do so.

A youngster will be able to be on his own in nursery school more comfortably if he has already grown accustomed to getting along without us from time to time and if he has had some experience in playing with other children. He may gain the courage to stay there without a parent with less anxiety if we assure him in words that we will come to get him at the end of the session. If someone else is to bring him home, we must be clear about who and how and tell him we will be at home waiting for him. If someone else is to be at home, we tell him who it will be, where we will be, and when we will see him again. The unknowns in the situation tend to make it more threatening. Sometimes mothers have found that leaving a scarf or a glove of theirs as a token that "I shall return" helps a forlorn three-year-old weather a morning without his mother.

The methods of fostering independence discussed in this chapter will contribute to a child's ability to use the facilities of nursery school, and that, in turn, increases his ability to act on his own in other situations.

How Much Independence Can He Take?

Various children are capable of varying degrees of independence at different ages. As we have seen, the cluster of traits and abilities we group together as "independent behavior" rest on how well a child can use his hands, how quickly or slowly he grasps a new idea and acts on it, how safe he feels in venturing on untried experiences, and how much trust he has in others and in himself. These abilities are rooted in his constitutional makeup, as well as the relationships and experiences he has known in his short life.

We can hardly decide arbitrarily how much independence to encourage or expect. We need to feed experiences to a three-, four-, or five-year-old bit by bit, giving him opportunity to experiment with self-reliance as we sense that he is ready to assume more.

Sometimes a boy or girl tells us in words, "I can do it myself," or "Let me do it myself," or "Don't hold me so tight." The latter phrase may literally refer to his hand being held as he walks on a walking beam, climbs a slide, or crosses the street, but it may also carry the hint that we can let go emotionally as well.

Sometimes boredom, restlessness, or even misbe-havior is an indication that a youngster can handle situations calling for greater self-sufficiency or skill. If, for instance, three-and-a-half-year-old Nicky "runs away" time after time, take a look at where he runs to. If his running away takes him to the group of children playing with obvious enjoyment down the block or across the street, he may be telling us that he is ready for more companionship and does not need to stay so close to home.

Sometimes the ease with which a child performs one act gives us a clue to a more complicated one he is ready to take on. For example, a three-year-old who has no trouble getting his clothes off is probably ready to learn how to put them on.

In offering opportunities for a youngster to attain the "I can do" feelings in an increasing number and variety of situations, we need to be alert to the cues he gives us. We can put some effort into being inventive in concocting ways for him to feel at once safe and independent, and be patient when he shows us that we have overestimated what he can do.

10

Minor Annoyances And Larger Worries

MORE PEOPLE, BOTH parents and professionals, are paying more attention to children and how they grow today than ever before in history. We may justifiably believe that we do better for the young than did earlier generations, in which small boys and girls were regarded as miniature adults or as being full of evil that had to be beaten out of them. At least we recognize that the world appears to three-, four-, and five-year-olds far different from the way it appears to adults, and that many of the minor annoyances in bringing up our sons and daughters stem from their misconceptions of the world around them.

Life in an industrialized society, especially in cities, is ill adapted to the needs of preschoolers. Our pattern of living and our values, as well as the lack of adequate health services, the lack of sufficient space, and the lack of enough adults who will take time to listen to youngsters deprive many of them of the opportunity to develop their potential for becoming creative, responsible, and responsive human beings. Many of our larger worries have their roots in these conditions.

Yet urban living may not be the only source of our vexations. On an unfrequented beach on the remote Pacific island of Bora Bora, this writer came upon a young mother, native to the island, and her two small daughters. The mother was braiding palm fronds into a lovely pattern to make a new wall for the thatched hut in which she and her husband lived in a clearing at the edge of the lagoon. She was trying to teach the elder of the girls how to hold the palm fronds and plait them without cutting her hands on the sharp edges. Her husband's fishing nets were drying nearby in the sun.

The scene seemed almost ideal for rearing happy children. No traffic hazards, plenty of sun, play space, sand and water, and no danger of disturbing the neighbors if the children's voices grew exuberantly noisy. Yet this young mother had as many complaints, and surprisingly familiar ones, as her counterparts in an apartment complex in a metropolitan area might have. She said that plaiting the palm fronds was rough and tedious work. Her daughter was clumsy and not interested in learning how to do it. Left alone with the two children while her husband fished on other beaches where the catch was better, she never got to the village, and she tired of having no one to talk to except the children. Our exchange of views took place in French, a language in which neither of us was exactly proficient, but there was no mistaking her meaning.

The aggravations that arise between parents and three- through five-year-olds are due, perhaps, as much to the human condition as to the pressures of our particular society. From Boston to Bakersfield to Bora Bora, the activities of the very young, if they are a parent's sole social diet, can be by turns wearing, threatening, and boring, although the children are at the same time endearing, amusing, and challenging. The demands that three-, four-, and five-year-olds make, early and late, not out of willfulness or lack of consideration, but out of their helplessness and immaturity, are often difficult to meet.

Not What You Do, but How You Do It, Counts

A degree of accommodation of one generation to another is called for, no matter where or how young children and their parents live together. What accommodations shall be made, and when and how, are questions that each family answers for itself according to its own tastes and tolerances. Strict or lenient styles in living may work out equally satisfactorily. How we feel about the restrictions we enforce or the freedom we encourage and what those regulations and privileges mean to the children influence the pattern and tone of family life more than do the rules or liberties themselves.

Children need to have their capacities taken into consideration, but mothers and fathers need not constantly make all the concessions. If, for instance, privacy and quiet are important to parents, they are not being rejecting or cold if they arrange some times when they are not to be disturbed, short of actual emergencies.

Small children can usually understand, if we take

the trouble to explain the situation, that grown people sometimes are tired, or do not feel well, or have work to do, and cannot always be ready to do what the children would like. A postponement of father's company will not be unbearable if a youngster has learned from experience that father says "Yes" to a request for his company or his help more often than he says "No." If father says, "Can't do it now, but we'll do it after supper," and remembers that commitment, his refusals in the future are easier to take.

When Piping Voices Become a Burden

"I wish I'd been a mother in the days when the rule was, 'Children should be seen and not heard'," remarked a young mother with three boys under the age of six.

To this young woman, the reverberation of small feet tramping up and down the hall, the shouts of brotherly arguments, or the slamming of doors all came under the head of "making a racket" and were acutely painful to her. Fortunately, she realized that if she was implacable about the level of clamor she permitted, she would have to be more elastic in other directions. Although it was sometimes difficult for her to do so, she shut her eyes to a certain amount of disorder and overlooked sketchily washed hands as a small price to pay for achieving the relative quiet that was necessary to her comfort.

One of the lessons preschoolers need to learn is that different occasions call for different kinds of behavior. Being noisy may be permissible outdoors, but not in the house. Indoors, talking or playing in the usual way may be approved from breakfast time on; but before the family's rising hour, although threes and fours may be wide awake, they are expected to keep quiet.

If two youngsters share a room and one of them habitually wakes early, it can be hard.

Ione, a lively three-year-old, was an early riser. Except in winter, when daylight came late, Ione was ready to begin the day before six in the morning. Her five-year-old sister, on the other hand, could sleep until almost half past seven, when their mother called them to get ready for breakfast. Ione seemed unable to remember what "being quiet" entailed. Singing or talking to herself as softly as she was able, pattering around the room to see if her favorite doll was where she left it the night before, opening drawers and cupboards, or standing at the side of her sister's bed and giving her an ever-so-gentle prod "to see if she is really sleeping or just pretending" were to Ione ways of being "very, very still." If Ione woke her sister, which happened about five days out of seven, the older girl would be grumpy. Then the two engaged in a noisy quarrel, which woke their parents, or became conspirators in mischief, which usually had the same effect.

Neither punishment nor reward served to keep Ione sufficiently quiet. Then her parents tried a new tack. At bedtime, Ione chose two or three toys that lent themselves to quiet play. These were put within easy reach so that she would not need to get out of bed to search for something to do when she woke up. Before her parents went to bed, they put a bread-and-butter sandwich on Ione's nightstand so that she could have "an all-by-herself picnic" if she was hungry when she awoke.

This routine did not work magic, but it did alleviate the situation. It kept Ione quieter, and because she stayed in her bed, she sometimes dozed off again.

Making a Game of Keeping Quiet

A game one mother found useful when banging and shouting became too much for her, or when she feared the din was disturbing her neighbors, was an invention she called "Mousy-quietness." The game might take the form of tiptoe, finger-on-lips follow-the-leader. Or it might be seeing if toys could be put away, with mother participating, without anyone making a sound. Again, the tiptoe routine supplied the fun. Sometimes she would have one youngster pantomime some activity, and anyone who recognized it could whisper his answer to the actor. Of course, the game usually ended with someone breaking out in giggles, but it did serve to lower the noise level for a time.

Children can be encouraged to keep their voices down by the example of parents who do not customarily shout. Small boys and girls tend to be better able to control their noise if at some time during the day they can be as unrestrainedly clamorous as young children occasionally need to be.

A small child *can* be taught to move quietly and keep his voice down, but the price of that teaching may be high. A divorced mother lived with her four-year-old son, Lawrence, on the third floor of a rambling old house owned by two elderly sisters, who were the only other occupants. Since one of the conditions on which the mother and her son became tenants was that the boy should not disturb the owners, quietness became the cardinal virtue for him.

Coming in from play (and even in the backyard, shouting was taboo), Lawrence would creep up the stairs and say proudly to his mother, "You couldn't hear me one bit, could you?" She would praise him for his good behavior and tell him that people liked a boy who didn't get in the way. (Hardly good mental hygiene, but pardonable under the circumstances.) Lawrence had few of the satisfactions that properly should be a four-year-old's lot, but he did derive a sense of achievement and power from being able to move so silently that nobody knew he was in the room.

The elderly ladies, encountering him in the kitchen, which his mother had the privilege of using, would say, "Larry is a good boy. He's never noisy." Then they might invite him to sit with them and watch television or surprise him with a treat of candy. Being quiet was the accomplishment that brought approval, and the message that came through to Lawrence was, "As long as you don't make a sound, people will like you." This led him to believe that to sit, undetected, behind a sofa or under a bed, listening to adult conversation, should be acceptable behavior. The old house had marvelous alcoves and walk-in closets where he could hide. When he did so in the rooms he and his mother occupied, she would laugh and tell him he was "a good hider," but if one of the elderly ladies found him, she would declare he was "a bad, sneaky boy."

The day he hid in the sisters' automobile and remained undiscovered until the two women reached their destination an hour from home, the less gentle of the two gave him a spanking. His mother also punished him for "being sneaky."

The moral of this story is that we can "overteach" a way of behaving so that a youngster believes that observing one rule is all that counts. At what point being quiet becomes being sneaky may seem clear enough to adults. To a small child who has no idea of the implications of not making one's presence known and who has had silence stressed, the situation becomes confusing.

"When kids make a noise, at least you know where they are, and that's worth a lot," an older woman frequently told her younger friends who complained of the din their children made.

A Time for Messiness

A time and place for legitimate use of sticky, gooey materials helps to keep messiness from spilling over and becoming more predominant than most adults find endurable. Small children love to handle moist, pliable substances. Adults, to whom such materials may be distasteful, tend to forget how children enjoy them. Clay and dough, mud and water, sand and finger paints are among the materials that offer threes and fours the chance to mess to their hearts' content. Some nursery school teachers would include tea teaves and coffee grounds among the materials that give variety to these tactile experiences, but only a few tolerant parents can encourage such experimentation.

With smock, apron, or bath towel to protect their clothes and several thicknesses of newspaper to cover the surface on which they work, youngsters can have their fill of squashing, pounding, shaping, and manipulating dough, clay, soapsuds, and the like. Finger paints and large sheets of brown wrapping paper or newsprint offer an excellent means of indulging the inclination to use spreadable substances and a gratifyingly wild mixture of colors.

"You may not put your hands in the mashed potatoes and mix them with the beets, but after lunch you can make something much prettier with finger paints (or paste and colored paper)," may be a kind of substitution acceptable to both four-year-olds and their parents.

A Time for Cleanliness

The avoidance of messiness, like the avoidance of noise, can be overemphasized, but some restrictions on continual slovenliness are wholesome. Hands can be washed before meals and after toileting. For those who enjoy going barefoot, a pail of water and a towel at the door, or just inside, to get feet reasonably clean before coming in the house, may be useful.

Preschoolers are sufficiently intrigued with lathering soap all over themselves to find baths acceptable, but routine hand-washing may be tedious. The stock answer to the directive, "Wash-up time, we're going to eat soon" is usually "I did wash." That may mean that washing took place half an hour or four hours ago, and whatever its efficacy at that time, a repeat performance is in order. We cannot expect young boys or girls to wash or comb their hair without reminders. When they do wash their hands and faces, threes and fours may become so involved in playing with soap and water or get their clothes so thoroughly splashed that supervision is needed to prevent undue messiness. Older children in the family can be effective supervisors.

Tooth-brushing may be so fascinating that, once reminded to embark on it, a small person may prolong the squeezing out of toothpaste, putting it on the brush, allowing it to fall off, and then starting the whole process over again without ever getting the brush in contact with his teeth. Such messiness needs to be stopped by saying, "You can squish your clay or your dough, but toothpaste is not to play with."

Cleanliness routines may become such a source of conflict at three or four that it may seem better, for the peace of the household, to keep them to a minimum for a time rather than endure the struggles and tears they produce. Five-year-olds can usually, with a few reminders, handle essential cleanliness measures fairly smoothly. These routines are also discussed in Chapter 9.

Cleanliness, a praiseworthy quality at the right time and place, can also be overdone. Some few children— and girls are more likely to be victims of this misfortune than are boys—learn all too well the lesson of not getting clothes dirty and of staying away from anything messy. Even sandbox play with wet sand becomes an activity from which the overclean shrink if they have found neatness and cleanliness the only way to a mother's heart.

The business of childhood is vigorous play. In these days of drip-dry clothes and sturdy fabrics meant to withstand grass stains, mud, and even grease, emphasis on spotlessness seems unnecessary and often works a hardship on a lively boy or girl.

One mother, who valued appearance above everything and took pride in seeing her attractive little girl look appetizingly fresh, would exclaim in disgust, "How did you manage to get *that* dirty so fast! Half an hour ago you were all nice and clean. What am I going to do with you?" Such statements, made time after time in a tone of stern disapproval, made her already timid daughter afraid of risking her mother's displeasure. So she stood on the sidelines, rarely joining in play and becoming more timid than ever.

Without spoiling a small child's zest for living or making him too conscious of dirt and germs, we can teach him not to pick up a piece of candy from the sidewalk and put it in his mouth, or accept the offer of a half-consumed lollypop. Small children touch everything and often taste it, too. Substances that we do not want them to taste or that are poisonous need to be kept out of reach, out of sight, and, in the case of medicines, under lock and key. Threes and fours do not understand the difference between, for example, not eating sugar out of the sugar bowl or drinking maple syrup and not tasting the powder that looks much like sugar or the liquid that has the appearance of maple syrup but is used to scrub the floor.

We need to make a distinction between what is prohibited on the grounds that it is sticky and messy and what is taboo because it is dangerous—and, for the sake of our child's future trust in us, we must be honest about which is which.

Perspective on the Amenities

In the same category as noise and dirt in many

homes is "bad language." Words that not long ago were banned have now become so common in print, in motion pictures, and in the conversation of many adults and older children that we can hardly be shocked if four-year-olds' vocabularies also include them. Yet four-year-olds have epithets of their own invention that still outrage many parents. To hear them saying, "You're a poo-poo," or "I'm going to put doo-doos all over you," or "I'm going to flush you down the toilet because you're a wee-wee" may not be shocking, but it can be tiresome to adults.

A certain amount of occupational deafness to such conversation may assist us in surviving until our youngster outgrows his flair for bathroom language and may hasten the day when he will relinquish it. One father's antidote for objectionable language was to suggest, "Wouldn't it be funnier to call your friend 'a broken old stove' than to use the words you use?" The father was aware that this brand of banter would not have the appeal to the small child, who is still interested in the products of his own body, that "bathroom talk" had, but it was in the long run a more serviceable way of attacking the problem than implying that the youngster's chosen vocabulary was "dirty." The child got the message that his father was not shocked by "bathroom words" but preferred that they not be used in his presence or that of other adults.

In dealing with objectionable language, too much noise, lack of neatness, or similar aggravations of pre-school behavior, we should keep in mind that these are quite usual problems of development. Almost every child will for a time be less clean, less well-spoken and mannerly than his parents might find convenient. But look at the whole child in the context of everything else he does. Is he usually happy and able to play with enthusiasm? Does he go fairly smoothly through most of the day's routines? Does he communicate with others freely and readily? If the answer to at least some of these questions is affirmative, we can afford to overlook, within the limits of our own tolerance, such typical preschool deviations from decorum as we have been discussing.

What Is the Whiner Trying to Tell Us?

On the borderline between a "minor annoyance" and a "larger worry" is the whining voice of a youngster who is usually discontented, frustrated, and provocative. Adults are often out of patience with him and as a result answer him curtly, insist that he repeat his statement in a more agreeable tone of voice, and generally add to his emotional discomfort.

Whining is usually a symptom, not the malady itself, and as such needs to be attacked indirectly. If we are confronted with a boy or girl whose customary tone is whining and complaining, we might ask ourself whether this youngster is receiving recognition and encouragement enough to convince him that he is a lovable, worthwhile individual? Does he have opportunities to make appropriate choices from time to time? Are the adults around him consistent in the limits they set for him? Do his parents take time to listen to him, play with him, enjoy his company and let him enjoy theirs? These questions may possibly uncover emotional needs that are not being adequately met and that are the source of his discontent.

Another thing to remember in trying to help a child whose frustration shows up in a whining tone of voice is that it undoubtedly took a long time for him to develop the whine (it is a mannerism that sneaks up on one), and it will not go away overnight.

Worries About Health

Emotional and physical well-being are so closely intertwined as to be inseparable. Feelings and bodily processes both respond to pressure. When a youngster's appearance or behavior seem to have gone askew, we must consider whether the cause of the trouble may be some infection or organic problem before we decide that "He is just stubborn," or trying to get attention, or scared by something. At the same time, before we decide that the medicine cabinet is our best ally, we might look at the events in his life that may have upset both feelings and physical functioning.

Feelings can no more be overlooked, if they are at the root of the trouble, than can a high fever or a painful sore throat. Like physical symptoms, disturbed feelings, which show up in many ways discussed in this volume, may need treatment from a qualified professional, a counselor in a family service agency, or a child therapist in private practice or in a child-guidance clinic.

A few boys and girls seem to go through the years of early childhood with such good health that their parents say, airily, "That one never gets sick." That state of affairs is less common than are occasional, perhaps slight, but worrisome and sometimes puzzling problems of physical well-being.

"Picky Eater"

One such problem is the disinterest in eating that besets many three- and four-year-olds. During these years, children often go through quite long spells when their appetites lag and eating seems a bore and a burden. They may have periods when they want raw vegetables and little else, or when bologna sandwiches are the only food they will touch. A youngster may eat ravenously for a few days and then have no appetite for a week.

Eating is not a moral issue, nor is a poor eater being defiant. We can accept the fact that appetite may be capricious. If its variations are not seen in terms of uncooperativeness and resistance, it tends to stabilize by the time a youngster is five or six.

Struggles over how much a child shall eat are useless, although in some families encouraging a child to "take a little taste of everything" seems to make for a more cosmopolitan palate. For one who is a slow eater, it is discouraging to have older members of the family finish eating and leave the table while he is still trying to plow through the food in front of him. Rather than be left to complete his meal alone, he may give up entirely and say he has had enough. It is possible that such a child is being served discouragingly large portions.

Breakfast may be by far the poorest meal of the day. The stand that "Everyone must have juice, a bowl of hot cereal, and egg and bacon to start the day" does not assist in cultivating the appetite of the three-year-old; and it is appetite, not will power or cooperation, that we are aiming for. Appetites tend to improve when mealtimes are pleasant and when the child does not get a mental picture of himself as someone who will not or cannot eat a large number of foods.

When Bowel and Bladder Control Lapse

Another difficulty during these years may be that the child who was apparently dependable about using the toilet and staying dry at night slips back into wetting and/or soiling. The occasional accidents in toileting that happen to many small boys and girls, because they put off toileting or are in an unfamiliar place and hesitate to ask where the bathroom is, are different from a complete breakdown in control. Sometimes a temporary lapse occurs because of a cold or other slight illness, but that, too, usually corrects itself if the youngster—and his parents—do not panic over it.

If the return to wetting or soiling has no medical basis—and the child's doctor is the one to make that decision—and if it is persistent, parents should consider the possible outside pressures that might be the source of the trouble.

A new baby in the family, arrivals or departures of other people important to the boy or girl, starting nursery school, or merely some event over which he or she is pleasantly excited may be the cause of a loss of nighttime bladder control and, less frequently, daytime control. The change in the household or in what is expected of him may be upsetting to the youngster because he must now be more "grown-up" than he feels capable of being. Loss of bladder control, especially at night, may be his unconscious protest against having to relinquish the privilege of being cared for.

"I know you don't want to wet your bed at night. Sometimes that happens to children when they are worried about something. If you talk about what is bothering you, you may feel better and be able to stay dry at night again," is an approach that may help. If a parent has a good idea of what is worrying a child, it might be mentioned as having caused other children to lose control for a time.

Some youngsters "forget" to use the toilet, and not simply because they are absorbed in play. Cliff was one who had never become quite reliable in the matter of going to the toilet when he needed to urinate, although he was nearly four. Cliff had been so hemmed in by prohibitions since babyhood that in desperation he usually resisted the signals from his own body that his bladder needed emptying, as well as commands from his parents. In Cliff's case, sessions at a child-guidance clinic, for him and for his parents, finally helped to change the attitudes in the family. Then Cliff no longer needed to defend himself from overwhelming demands by constantly resisting.

When the cause of not acquiring or not maintaining control of elimination is deep-seated resistance, other unacceptable behavior is usually also present. Here, again, we need to put in focus everything that is happening to the youngster and try to meet the problem as a whole, rather than resorting to a gimmick that attacks only part of the difficulty. Some of the suggested remedies for lack of complete control may be far too hard on the child. For example, denying him fluids from late afternoon until bedtime in the hope that it will cut down nighttime wetting may make a child miserably thirsty. Punishment or shaming only add to his discouragement, which is probably already acute. Expressing confidence that he can and will do better, occasionally reminding, but not nagging, are aids to a youngster's own inner controls.

If a really disheartening situation has developed, either because control has not been established or because it has broken down completely, psychological help may be needed.

The subject of toileting is also considered in Chapter 9. Sara Gilbert's *Three Years to Grow* gives sound information on teaching your child to use the toilet.

Will Poor Speech Be Outgrown?

Among other babyish kinds of behavior that often persist is poor enunciation. Three-year-olds are not likely to have perfect pronunciation, but the five- or five-and-a-half-year-old usually is readily understandable. If a child is developing well in most directions, is alert and interested in his play and in trying to use language, the inability to pronounce one or two sounds clearly at the age of three or even four and a half is not serious. The substitution of the sound "w" for the sound "l", resulting in such confusing statements as "We had wiver for wunch," will probably correct itself if a youngster hears the correct sound.

Parents and older brothers and sisters should avoid falling into the trap of adopting the three-year-old's mispronunciation in fun. Children learn from good models in speech as in other matters. The small one's style of talking may be ever so endearing, but his family help him most by using correct speech sounds.

Many three-year-olds, when they are excited, may not be able to get their words out smoothly. They hesitate over the initial sounds, and their parents may believe they have a stutterer on their hands. That type of stutter we can afford to ignore, as it usually disappears before a child is old enough to go to school.

Persistent inability in a child of four and a half or five to start a word without repeating the initial sounds, or spasmodic repetition of sounds whenever he speaks, is usually a sign of anxiety, if no physical impediment in his vocal apparatus is present. Trying to find and ease the source of that anxiety is what is needed, not making a child repeat what he has said or calling attention in any way to his defective speech.

Some children stutter or stammer only when they are in new situations or with strangers. In a study of children who stutter, researchers found that parents of stutterers were less realistic in what they expected of their children (in other words, set standards too high) than were the parents of nonstutterers. Another study, comparing a group of young boys who stuttered with a group that did not, found that the mothers of stutterers tended to "reject their children more often than they accepted them, while the mothers of a similar group of boys who did not stutter accepted their children more often than they rejected them."

Many schools, hospitals, and clinics have speech therapists on their staffs who can help children who have marked and continual difficulty in speaking.

Size and Weight as Signs of Healthy Growth

Parents are often concerned because they are not

sure how much a child should be growing during these years. Obviously, if growth did not slow down after the first six months of a baby's life, we would be a race of giants. Individual rates of growth vary tremendously. Two preschoolers of the same age may differ by as much as five inches in height or fifteen pounds in weight and yet both be within the range of normal and be perfectly healthy.

A gain of three to six pounds and two to four inches in a year is evidence that a youngster is growing satisfactorily. It may be interesting and useful to keep a semiannual record of a child's weight and height as documentary proof of progress. If a change of doctor or clinic becomes necessary, such a record also may be appreciated by the new medical adviser.

"Bigger" does not necessarily mean "healthier" or "stronger." Indeed, the conspicuously overweight child is at a disadvantage on several counts. He is likely to be awkward and to be the butt of his playmates' ridicule. From a health point of view, overweight, even at an early age, is generally regarded by the medical profession as a potential hazard.

Healthy Attitudes Toward Health

By the time a child is three, parents have usually discovered the tempo and general behavior that signify that a particular youngster is well or that he may be "coming down with something."

The mother of a lively brood says, "When one of our children walks when he could run or sits when he could stand, I can be pretty sure he'll have a fever by evening. In this house, who needs a thermometer?"

She may be exaggerating the validity of her hunches, but a sharp change in a child's level of energy or in his color or general bearing is not to be overlooked.

For reasons we cannot always understand, some children are more susceptible than others to colds, sore throats, stomach upsets, or elevations in temperature. Such susceptibility is worth reporting to the doctor when we take that child for a checkup, but not in the child's hearing. We should avoid letting the youngster get the impression that he is fated to be ill frequently, or letting it be said in the family or among the neighbors that "He (or she) always gets everything. Poor kid, just has no resistance." The doctor may have recommendations about diet or routines or some special measures that will help to give the susceptible child a better chance of fighting off slight but bothersome illnesses.

If a child seems likely to contract minor illnesses, we may need to protect him from becoming overtired or from whatever seems to put a strain on him. If he is allergic to certain foods or other substances, we should try to help him avoid them without letting him become unduly concerned about his health.

"Everybody has something he can't do," a father with an asthmatic daughter told her. "You can't eat eggs and white bread. O.K. Brother can't see to read in school if he forgets his glasses. When I was little I had to wear special shoes that laced up when the other kids were wearing sneakers. Everybody has to take care sometimes." Such an attitude helps a child feel he is not odd because he must observe a few restrictions.

Children have a strong drive toward health. They

tend to respond to sound medical treatment and also to bounce back from an illness quickly. We can cooperate with their tendency to be well by using all the means at our disposal to prevent or remedy any impairments. We can give our children the point of view that most youngsters usually feel well, but if they do get sick, something can be done about it.

When to Consult the Doctor?

When a child is sick, there is no substitute for professional skill and diagnosis. Medical science may not always have a ready and complete answer, but intelligent parents realize how infinitely superior it is to the counsel of even an experienced relative or neighbor. When a child runs a high fever, vomits repeatedly, complains of a severe pain, coughs hard and continually, or acts in a manner so unlike his usual self that common sense tells us he is sick, we want medical help and we want it as promptly as possible. Even a mild illness that lasts more than two or three days is not to be ignored.

Keeping a sick child quiet, warm, and on a bland diet until we can get in touch with the doctor or clinic is sensible. Unless the doctor has given specific directions about medication to be given when certain symptoms appear in a particular child, it should be a rule not to do amateur prescribing.

Another aspect of the question of when to consult the doctor concerns the time of day chosen for getting in touch with him. Many pediatricians instruct the parents of their patients that they prefer to be called on the telephone during certain hours.

A mother may tend to wait until her husband

comes home in the evening so that they can decide together about phoning their pediatrician or taking the youngster to his office or to the clinic. From the standpoint of family solidarity, that is fine; but from the practical point of view of both the child's well-being and the doctor's convenience, a mother might do better to report the condition while the doctor is still at his office.

The decision to take a child to the doctor may need to be made because of some persistent and increasing sign of poor health. Perhaps we suspect that a boy's or girl's hearing is not what it should be, even allowing for children's inattention to what they don't want to hear. Perhaps a cough has hung on far too long to be attributed to the damp weather and the fact that "colds are harder to shake off this year." Listlessness and vague pains, a sharp decrease in appetite, and a willingness to stay in bed cannot be overlooked in a five-year-old who, up to a few weeks ago, was full of energy. In these and similar instances, the doctor will appreciate having the youngster brought to his office promptly. The sooner steps are taken to correct whatever the condition may be, the more effective treatment can be.

When Keeping Records Pays

No matter how casual we may be about writing most things down, it is well worthwhile to keep careful records of the dates of the inoculations our children have had and who administered them. In Sara Gilbert's book, *Three Years to Grow*, there is a chart of childhood diseases that confer immunity, the inoculations a child should have, and the times at which such immunization needs to be given. This chart can help to avoid omitting any of the available and proven preventive measures for protecting a child.

Parents may say, "We all had measles (or scarlet fever, or whatever it may be) in our family when we were kids, and we survived just fine. I can't believe all those shots are necessary." But this is a shortsighted line of reasoning. A light case of a childhood disease that is now preventable may have been survived (if survival is all one is concerned about) by millions of children in the past, but there is no sense in risking the complications and/or damage to vital organs that may come in the wake of those illnesses.

We may be sure we will never forget the contagious illnesses or the immunizations our children have had, but we may not be available when that information is needed. Such data had best be recorded.

How Much Television for Young Children?

Television-viewing in some families becomes a facet of daily life that qualifies as "a worry"—and no wonder, when, according to a careful study, the average American child between the ages of three and sixteen spends one sixth of his waking hours in front of the television set.

Television is a source of information and entertainment that enriches life in many directions, but we need to learn to use it with discrimination. Keeping a television set going all day long without regard for what program is on the screen wastes time that might be spent more constructively.

Almost every TV station provides some programs that are suitable for the young. Television-viewing can be a pleasant treat for a youngster if he watches two or three programs in the course of a day. But such viewing tends to lose its flavor if it is his only way of spending his time. As for permitting preschoolers to watch adult programs indiscriminately, is there any logic in allowing the emotional strain of seeing a procession of incomprehensible and often disturbing situations?

"I keep the TV on, but our youngsters don't just sit and watch it. They are playing and talking and really don't pay much attention to it," say some parents. Then why, if no one is really watching it, should it be turned on? We are subjected to sufficient noise in the course of the day without the jangle and jabber of unwatched programs.

A research study has documented some effects of TV on young children. The hours they spend in viewing must be taken from other activities. Some are taken from sleep and some from what the study described as "casual play." We may interpret casual play as the ability to fill in an odd quarter of an hour with enjoyable, reasonably constructive, perhaps creative activity on their own. It is this cultivation of one's own resources that tends to wither when television is omnipresent. Some mothers insist, "But it keeps them out of mischief and they don't make all kinds of a mess getting out toys that they play with ten minutes and then leave. Whatever else it does, TV saves me a lot of work." There is no denying that argument, but without being hard on busy mothers we might suggest that a toy-strewn room may mean "Children growing here," whereas one in perfect order with a three- and five-year-old glued to the TV set may indicate a sterile life for the youngsters.

Several studies have indicated that viewing an aggressive film on TV does not drain off and reduce aggression in a youngster as effectively as does channeling angry feelings through direct and legitimate action. Such an active outlet might be punching an inflated plastic figure or engaging in games that involve running, climbing, and jumping.

What Is "Too Much" TV?

When a youngster becomes so addicted to television that it is the only activity he enjoys, when he rarely, if ever, turns to any kind of spontaneous play, then we may suspect that he is escaping from an existence that holds no other gratifications. The five-year-old who, when asked what he likes to do, replies, "Watch TV. What else?," has probably been permitted an overdose. Perhaps too many restrictions or lack of parental ingenuity have made him hesitate to spend his time in other pursuits that children this age can find satisfactory.

For such young TV addicts, limiting the hours of viewing is usually only a partial solution and less effective than examining the total picture of the boy's or girl's relationships and surroundings. Perhaps what is needed is more opportunities to play with other children, in an organized group or nursery school, or in his home or theirs. More time with his parents or more recognition and encouragement might generate incentive to try other activities.

It is probably easier to wean a three-year-old or a five-year-old from TV addiction than an older child. "He will outgrow spending hours watching," is usually an unfounded hope. If parents believe their son's or daughter's TV-watching pattern needs to be modified, they can make the change gradually. They may need to start by modifying their own watching pattern, turning the set on only for a program they really want to see.

Just how many programs a three-, four-, or five-year-old may watch without becoming an "addict" depends less on the quality of the programs, or even the actual time devoted to viewing, than on what he does when he is not parked in front of the television set. If TV is only one of a number of his interests, then one cartoon more or less is not crucial.

Inevitably, in addition to watching the programs that are suitable for him, the preschooler will often be in the room when other members of the household are watching their favorites or listening to news reports. At such times it can help to get the youngster started on some kind of play he particularly likes.

TV Versus Being Read To

Television as a force in the lives of our children is here to stay, but it is no substitute for the warmth and closeness of human relationships. One of the ways in which such warmth comes through to small children is cuddling up to a friendly grown-up and listening to the reading or telling of a well-loved story or verse. The most aesthetic and delightful TV program cannot take the place of those homely, plotless, highly personalized tales made up for the benefit of the three- or four-year-old and featuring him as the principal character. The story usually begins: "Once there was a little girl named Beverly." At this point the child interrupts to say, "Just like my name!" The tale goes on to reveal where Beverly lived and what she and the other members of the family did each hour of the day. The real Beverly listens more entranced than by a well-plotted, beautifully written masterpiece. She is likely to prompt the storyteller if he is so careless as to omit detailing what

Beverly had for supper or what color her bedroom slippers were.

Children who have the kind of relationship with parents or grandparents fostered by such moments together, and for whom being read to is a frequent and happy experience, will be less prone to TV addiction. They will probably still enjoy television, but being read to and hearing stories will be a good balance to the time spent at the TV set.

Worries and Annoyances in Perspective

Vexations and anxieties over children's development, their health, or the way they spend their time are neither new nor confined to the United States. In spite of the study that has been devoted to children's behavior in the past half century, we still cannot set down a blueprint for the optimum development of the preschooler. But this much we do know: the crucial question is not "Do I have annoyances and worries over my youngsters?" but rather, "How am I doing with the inevitable problems that crop up?" As has been emphasized throughout this chapter, we must try to see the whole child, rather than a specific problem. If problems are to be kept to manageable proportions, we must try to balance, sometimes to juggle, the children's needs with our own. At some points, adult needs will take priority, but in other circumstances the youngster's requirements will come first. Our goal is not to get rid of all conflicts and aggravations, but to accept, live with, and try to work through problems without letting them seriously interfere with either our enjoyment of the children or the satisfactions the children find in life.

11

Preparing Your Child For School

Preparation for school goes on throughout the first five or six years of a child's life. Sometimes parents take explicit steps to provide experiences or information to further this preparation. More often it is woven into the fabric of daily life without anyone's being aware of what is taking place. Whether a child is "well prepared" or "ill prepared" depends on intangible attitudes and relationships as well as on what parents may say or do. A child's own unique constitution and all the events in his brief past influence how he will assimilate the preparation his parents provide.

Starting "real school," which usually means first grade, is a milestone, despite the fact that a six-year-old may already have had a year of kindergarten and have attended nursery school as well. The child who lives in a school district that has no kindergarten may enter first grade having had no previous contact with anything

275

resembling a scheduled school day.

A population survey quoted recently in *The New York Times* found that one in every five children of three and four years of age was enrolled in some kind of established nursery school. Still, the difference between a neighborhood nursery school, conducted in a casual manner, and a large, rather formal kindergarten in a public school is often more marked than the difference between kindergarten and first grade. Whether the big change in a child's life comes when he goes to kindergarten or starts first grade, attending a school that houses, in the same building, classes for the "big kids" is a great event.

Parents are not immune to the excitement, tinged with apprehension, that pervades the atmosphere as opening day approaches. The chill some of them feel in the air that September morning is not owing entirely to a seasonal drop in temperature. Now their youngster will be on his own as he never has been before. Parents sense the challenge to their offspring, and indirectly to them. They will be judged by how this child performs.

Most mothers, and some fathers, are poignantly aware that early childhood, when parents are the unrivaled models and arbiters, tends to end at the classroom door. From here on, increasingly, "what my teachers says" and "what the other kids do" will compete with the wisdom mother and father dispense. The values and standards of home will remain strong in the primary grades and usually will win out in the long pull, but questioned they will often be. That is a sobering thought when "Get ready for school" advertisements fill the newspapers.

What Does "Getting Ready for School" Mean?

When we think of getting our son or daughter ready for school, our first thought may be of new shoes and alterations on "hand-me-down" skirts or pants. Then there are visits to the family doctor or a clinic or specialists to have sight and hearing checked. Discovering any defects and correcting them before a child enters school can prevent unnecessary confusion and frustration for him as he is required to use his eyes and ears in unaccustomed ways.

Parents may eagerly drill their young in writing their names, recognizing letters, reciting the alphabet, counting. Some schools discourage this. Many educators insist that although some boys and girls learn to read almost spontaneously and holding them back would be foolish, the pushing of sheer memorizing is at best a waste of effort and may even prejudice a boy or girl against learning.

What, then, are the attitudes and the skills, the abilities and the facts that can be absorbed at home in the years before five and six that will make a child a better "learner" and lay the foundation for his profiting from and enjoying his formal education? How do parents create a setting for learning?

In their concern with making sure their children learn certain facts or skills, parents may overlook important facets of the youngster's education in the years from three to six. Both learning and education go on in and out of school at any age, and it may be useful to define and distinguish between them.

Dr. René Spitz, in a recent paper, *Fundamental Education*, explains that "Education, by changing the person himself, becomes a permanent part of the personality." Learning is an important branch of education, but it is not the whole story. What one learns is stored, through a complicated process, in a "memory bank." To preserve what one has learned, one must use it, for without the reinforcement of practice and use, a skill or a body of information will, as Dr. Spitz puts it, "be subject to the wear and tear of life . . . deteriorate and disappear."

Education Is Not Just School

In this broader sense, "education" is not just having gone to school. It is the effect that all one's experiences and relationships—all the learning one has done in school and out—have had on the way one tackles a problem, responds to other people, forms judgments, or expresses feelings. Education affects what we are. Learning affects what we know.

As an example of this distinction, consider what takes place when a child first recognizes letters. He may be delighted and amazed that all the road signs having the letters "s-t-o-p" have the same meaning. Picking out the word "stop" becomes a fascinating game. A wider world begins to open up. Yet, let us suppose an impossible situation. If this child were to have no more experience with reading, never see another written word, he would, in all likelihood, forget the combination of lines and curves that signify the word he has learned to read.

Now consider a youngster who has had scant acquaintance with picture or story books. Then, at school, at the home of a friend, or in his own home, he is read to by someone he cares for. This person is also fond of him and likes reading to children. Through being read to, he discovers the joy of imagining, along with the author, delightfully impossible creatures, landscapes, or events; of hearing about children like himself or those quite different; of reveling in nonsense or the rhythms of verse. He is attracted at first to being read to because someone whom he admires is paying attention to him. Clearly, that person likes reading. Right here is a motive for his becoming involved with stories and books.

Being read to usually, but not invariably, seems preferable to watching television, listening to the radio, or going to a movie, because when he is read to, he has not only the story but also the person reading it to interest him. Books have entered his life as a source of pleasure. Gradually, sometimes quite suddenly, being read to becomes a resource to rescue him from the sulks or doldrums. His personality has expanded. He will hardly be the same again!

Such an experience is "education," since while the material he learns through being read to may or may not stay with him, the taste for listening to poems and stories, and later for reading on his own, is permanent and is, incidentally, excellent preparation for school. If books have been a source of pleasure at home, then using them in school will tend to be gratifying.

What Does It Take to Learn?

Social and emotional well-being and readiness to learn are vital aspects of being prepared for first grade.

In recent years, attention has been paid to the fact that whereas some children come to school eager to

learn, others are so blocked, so unable to grasp or disinterested in grasping subject matter as to be judged
mentally deficient by their teachers. Further study of
some of these children revealed that, long before they
reached first grade, events in their lives, rather than
their lack of native endowment, had dulled their ability
to assimilate information and make it a part of themselves.

Given a boy or girl who is not indeed mentally
handicapped, how he will respond to his teachers and
their teaching is largely determined by his attitude
toward himself and other people, particularly those in
authority, his feeling about trying anything new, and
his parents' attitudes about schools and learning.

The basic ingredients of the "mix" for learning and
for absorbing education are a part of that sequence in
development that has been described in earlier chapters.
Against the background of being prepared for school,
these developmental steps may take on added significance. They are worth reviewing in this light.

Learning takes confidence and courage. The foundation for these qualities is laid down in infancy. The
baby who feels comfortable much of the time, whose
mother is generally reliable about feeding him when he
is hungry and satisfying his need for affection, develops
trust in that good mother. His feeling, long before he
understands language, is, "She is good. She is good to
me. Therefore I am good."

Giving Baby the Right Start

Babies who develop trust in the person who takes
care of them in their first year have a start toward liking

themselves and trusting others. Five or six years later they will be likely to regard teachers as persons potentially friendly who will be helpers, not capricious tyrants. Trust, of course, will need to be seasoned with judgment as a child grows, because utter, blind trust would make no sense in many situations.

Out of trust in themselves comes enough confidence for babies to reach out, use their senses, and become acquainted with their world. Learning at any age and in many situations calls for reaching out boldly with one's mind and with one's senses. Good mothering in early life is basic for good learning later on.

Also necessary for learning is a nice blend of the ability to move about independently, to control oneself in some degree, and at the same time to accept a measure of control from others. Maintaining self-regulation and acquiescing to regulation from outside is one of the directions in which a child grows during his second year. If his development is proceeding in healthy fashion, he is keenly aware that he is a self-propelling individual.

Three- and four-year-olds, as every parent knows, are full of curiosity. They take the initiative, as has been explained earlier, in making discoveries. They speak out frequently—sometimes, it seems, continually. Exploring and speaking up are excellent ways to learn in many situations, but *only* using initiative and expressing feelings would hardly be an appropriate approach for every situation. Initiative will, from time to time, in even a single day, run afoul of necessary adult restrictions and need to be curbed and redirected. When that happens, a small child feels guilty. We have seen earlier in this book that guilt in small doses can temper curiosity and make for a healthy conscience. (See also Chapters 1, 7, and 9 on this subject.)

These same ingredients, *if they are in a proper balance*, are also an aid to learning. To what degree too much guilt can impede experimentation and learning is illustrated by an answer a three-and-a-half-year-old in nursery school gave. The little girl was painting with blue and yellow paint. Her teacher noticed that the girl was mixing the two colors. Since this child was extremely timid and seldom ventured to try anything she had not explicitly been told to do, the teacher, in a most encouraging manner, said, "Cindy, what do you get when you mix blue and yellow?"

"You get a whipping," was Cindy's answer, distilled out of three years of harsh repression that had made her all but inaccessible to the warmth the teacher offered.

Children who have not been mistreated as Cindy had, but have been able to work successfully through each step in development, have gone a long way in "learning how to learn." Their energies are not frittered away in anxiety but can be mobilized to master a subject and grapple with an unfamiliar problem, be it sounding out a word or following directions when the class goes on a field trip. These children have gained approval for making a bold attempt in the past. They feel "it is safe to learn." That which is new is not bound to be painful, but can be pleasant. The opposite of Cindy's plight was the happy approach of a five-year-old boy whose usual response to suggestions made by his teacher was, "O.K. That'll be great. I'll try it."

Parents may resent being told, when they are looking for a means of instilling those concrete abilities that
will help their sons and daughters become good students, that confidence, the capacity to move about
independently, to control bodily functions, and accept
directions, together with a willingness to risk taking the
initiative in exploring surroundings, are the foundations
for effective learning in school. Indeed, it would be
easier were there an exercise, a sort of "intellectual
push-up," that could be practiced daily and that would
guarantee the mastery of reading and writing in first
grade!

Parents need to recognize that because they play
such a vital part in the development of their children's
feelings and ability to live with others, they are usually
too involved with their offspring to make the best
teachers of reading and writing.

In a paper entitled *Parents and Teachers—Who
Does What?* Dr. Rudolph Eckstein points out:

There must be bringing up that is based on [pa-
rental] love . . . and there must also be bringing up
in terms of a love which allows for distance. For
this reason parents, even if they are good teachers,
don't make good teachers [of school subjects] of
their own children. . . . Every one of us, even if he
is a fine teacher otherwise and has all the patience
in the world for learning processes, finds that it
breaks down at home. . . . If it didn't break down,
it would only function because one would be so
distant from the children that one relates to them
as if they were students. . . . Parents and teachers

. . . have two different functions: the teaching that comes out of intimacy, of closeness, . . . and the kind of distant love and distant teaching that is typical of the school system.

A Child Needs to Like Himself in Order to Learn

The hard fact is that children who have self-respect, who believe in their own worth, whose curiosity has not been brutally squelched, have a head start in school over those who are afraid to try out their abilities or to trust anyone because the results of doing either have only been more hurts, as was the case with Albert.

Albert's mother had died when he was an infant. He had been cared for, or more often not cared for, by a succession of relatives who found the droopy, whining boy unappealing and burdensome. When his father remarried, the stepmother took a dim view of the boy and gave him as little attention as possible.

If Albert, when he was four or five, asked a question or asked for help, which he seldom dared do, the response was usually a flat "Shut up. Get out of my way," or perhaps a less quotable admonition. If he had the bad luck to irritate his stepmother, she locked him in a dark closet. The father found the new wife no more likable than did the boy, but the father could— and did—walk out on the situation.

When her husband left, the stepmother lost no time in placing Albert in a foster home. That was the last he saw of her. By the time he was of an age for first grade (to say he was "ready" would be too optimistic), Albert had known three foster homes of varying quality, besides having had two stays in the county institution for dependent and neglected children.

A few months before he turned six, he had been placed with patient and kindly foster parents, but the damage done to him had been so great that it was not to be repaired quickly, if at all. He was destructive, suspicious, unwilling to talk or to cooperate. Everything that had happened had told him he was a worthless nuisance.

Going to school meant to him encountering one more set of persons who would make demands he could not meet. He could not have put those feelings into words, but they were, nonetheless, his response to the classroom.

Albert, and thousands of children like him, have trouble in school and fail to learn, not because they have learned nothing before they entered first grade, *but because they have learned the wrong things too well,* as Robert Hess points out in a study on learning. The lessons of their lives have instilled apathy, fear, and defiance.

Learning blocks also occur in children whose experiences have not been harsh, but who are, for some reason less easily detected, short on self-confidence.

This discussion of what interferes with learning may serve to highlight the self-esteem, the faith in others, and the zest for living that are a sound foundation for the early grades.

Telling It Like It Is

A parent's own feelings about schools and teachers influence his child's attitude toward learning. Few parents today would use school as a threat, although in a moment of exasperation with an uncooperative five-year-old they might, as one mother did, exclaim, "Just you wait until you get to school. Your teacher won't let you get away with acting like that." Of course, picturing schools as institutions specializing in punishment sours the young on them immediately.

Often, the tendency of well-intentioned parents is to go too far in the opposite direction: "School will be fun. You'll have friends your own age to play with. You'll learn to read and write and do all sorts of interesting things. Isn't it exciting to be a big boy and go to a real school?"

Yet such a rosy view hardly squares with the real state of affairs. If we put ourselves in our youngster's place and recall how we felt on the momentous day when we entered first grade, we will probably remember that we had some misgivings. Perhaps we were afraid of making some mistake that would betray our bewilderment. We may have imagined everyone else knew exactly what to do and we alone were worried about finding our way home at noon, finding the toilet room, or remembering to bring a dime tomorrow, although we did not understand why we were to bring it.

If we thought about our younger brothers and sisters safely at home with mother, having a mid-morning snack in the familiar kitchen, tears of loneliness may have filled our eyes. The teacher may have talked too fast for us to understand what she was saying. All these and many other circumstances may have made our first days at school less than pleasant.

Even if we can bear to summon up memories that may have been long buried, we may elect not to discuss our own childhood feelings with our first-grader-to-be, lest we create anxiety where it need not exist. Yet, does anyone really escape having some bad moments? In discussing the desirability of being honest, rather than overselling school, Dr. Norman Paul, writing on "Parental Empathy" in *Parenthood—Its Psychology and Psychopathology*, says:

The child finds school terrifying or restrictive or both, and concludes that he must somehow be inadequate. Didn't his parents imply it would be exciting and pleasant? Is there something wrong with him because he dreads the ringing of the school bell, finds the teacher a big, threatening person, and distrusts all the children who sit around him? Although he is experiencing the very feelings that many others have experienced, he is left with an impression of aloneness in his trouble. Ashamed of his inadequacy, he pretends at home that all is well. The parents are relieved that he has already adjusted to school. And the whole painful process of getting used to the new life is submerged in silence. . . . And so each child is left to traverse life's problems alone, as though his responses were so unique and uncharacteristic that they must be kept private.

Perhaps parents, in presenting what school will be like, might take the line Mrs. Hansen followed:

You'll have lots of different feelings about school; at least I know I did, and your Daddy says he did, too. Sometimes it will be fun, but other days maybe you won't like it so much. Right at first, you may not have many friends, or even know the other children. The boys and girls on our block whom you play with may not be in the same classroom you are. The funny thing is that probably all the other children feel the same way you do. They want to make friends, but they feel strange, too. We can always talk about it if something at school bothers you or you don't understand what your teacher wants you to do. You go to school to learn lots of interesting things, but that takes a long time. You'll be a good learner.

Can Children Understand the "Dailiness" of School?

If we are to be realistic in talking about first grade, two points probably need to be made clear. That many children have misconceptions about these two points is demonstrated by two anecdotes that have become folklore. The first concerns the child who returned home at the end of his first day at school in a rage: "That old dump of a school is no good. You said I'd learn to read and I was there all day and I didn't learn anything. I'm never going back again."

The other story concerns a six-year-old who had looked forward to going to school for months and had gone with enthusiasm on the first day; but, when her mother told her it was time to get up and dress for school the next morning, she said, "What? Not again! I went to school yesterday!"

We need to emphasize to the children the gradualness of learning to read, to write, to add, or to do the other things one learns in first grade. We can prevent keen disappointment if we explain this carefully along with the statement that one goes to school for a long time.

Mothers Interpret the Teacher's Role

In addition to giving children a candid but encouraging view of school, parents need to think carefully about how they explain what a teacher does. A teacher is neither another mother or father nor a policeman. He or she is a giver of information and the ultimate authority in the classroom. Without making teachers seem a stern and forbidding breed, this can be put in words a six-year-old can understand:

> In school you do what the teacher tells you to, just the way Daddy and I expect you to do what we ask you to do at home. You can always ask your teacher if you don't know what to do or don't know what she means when she tells you something.

Such an attitude reassures a child that he will have a source of help when he is a stranger in a strange place, and also lets him know there will be limits on what is permitted.

For a variety of reasons, not all parents offer an encouraging picture of first grade. Some are more concerned that their children behave than that they have a satisfying learning experience. Sometimes, in metropolitan neighborhoods, real hazards exist for the small child who goes back and forth to school on streets where older children may threaten him or do him physical harm. Some families may feel that their children will not be given a fair chance by teachers or other children. If the schools have become a pawn in a struggle for power in the community, parents may fear their child will have only mediocre instruction. When such conditions exist, parents find it difficult, if not impossible, to reassure their children that going to school will be, on the whole, interesting, safe, or rewarding. Perhaps the best one can do under such circumstances is to stress that "Lots of people are trying to make things better, and some teachers are going to be friendly to you."

Various Approaches Taken by Parents

How different parents present school to their children has been brought out in a study carried on at the University of Chicago by Robert Hess, Ph.D., and Virginia Shipman. Mothers from various neighborhoods were asked what they would tell their six-year-olds before they went to school for the first time.

Some mothers stressed obedience to the teacher and the need "to be nice and quiet, and listen." Others stressed safety in crossing the streets on the way to and from school. Still others said they would talk about what the child would learn in school. Some, probably themselves frightened by the entire idea of school, said they would reassure the youngster that he could come home again and that mother would pick him up when school was out.

Clearly, the concerns and anxieties of these mothers colored their children's ideas of what might go on in school. The emphasis in many of the replies was on what a child would need to beware of, with no mention of the satisfactions that might also exist.

Reading what these mothers said, one realizes that the human tendency is to present only one facet of schools and teachers, which can give a child a lopsided view of what he will do in school.

Few mothers gave as well-rounded a picture as the one who said:

First of all, I would take him to see his new school. We would talk about the building, and after seeing the school I would tell him that he would meet new children who would be his friends and that he would work and play with them. I would explain that the teacher would be his friend, would help him and guide him in school, and that he should do as she tells him to.

Seeing Is Believing, So Take a Look

A visit to the school is certainly desirable. Some schools do arrange for parents to have a conference with their child's teacher before opening day. Mothers bring their children along, giving teachers and pupils a chance to have a look at one another. The child who has seen the classroom, the corridors, and—not to be overlooked —the washroom will feel less strange when he enters as a pupil.

Some suburban schools and schools in small communities plan for first-grade teachers to make home visits, if classes are not so large as to make this impracticable. A few parents object to these visits as "prying," but usually the teachers are welcomed. It is one way to avoid having meetings with the teacher come about only when something has gone wrong.

Any plan that offers an opportunity for the pupil and his mother to come to the school and discover how the day is spent and who will be in charge is a definite advantage for everyone involved. One father relates:

> The best thing my father did for me before I started school was to walk with me, not once but lots of times, over the route I'd take to and from school each day. That gave me a thread for finding my way back, in every sense of the word, and being sure I knew how to get home again kept me on solid ground for the first few days when I might have panicked, as I was small and scared and, I suppose, overprotected.

Separation Takes Practice

One form of overprotection that may make going to school harder for a six-year-old is not having become accustomed to being away from his mother for a day, or part of a day. This happened to Bea, and it resulted in her spending the first few weeks in school either crying quietly or sitting in a tense and depressed state, unable to take in what was going on around her. Bea's parents had moved many times from one city to another and from one neighborhood to another since she had been born. Neither her mother nor father was quick to make friends. They were far from relatives and were too proud or too shy to ask favors from casual acquaintances. As a result, they had no one to whom they could say, "Will you take our children for an afternoon?" When the mother went to the hospital for the birth of Bea's two younger sisters, her father took his vacation time and stayed home. Bea had never learned, through pleasant times with adults other than her parents, that others would and could take good care of her. The message that came through from her mother's constant presence was, "You could not get along without me, so I will not leave you even for a day." Although leaving her children with someone else occasionally might not have been easy to arrange, the obstacles to doing so were not as insuperable as Bea's mother believed them to be.

Independence develops as preschool children have the opportunity to practice it. Separations, in small doses, can prove it is safe, even enjoyable.

"The World Is So Full of a Number of Things"
When we take our children on excursions to the zoo or the airport; to see a farm or for a ride on a bus (or, if we can find one, a train); to a museum if one is nearby; to the fire station or to the library to select a book; to watch a house being built or a sidewalk repaired, we may not think of it as preparation for school. Yet such experiences, in digestible portions, give children a background of information and assurance. They tie in with topics that will be talked about in first grade. What is more, on such excursions a youngster acquires the manners needed for enjoying oneself without infringing on the rights of others in public places.

He usually can learn through these experiences whom to ask for information if it is needed; what to do if he is separated from the adults in charge of him; what it means to wait one's turn in line and why that is necessary sometimes; how one buys a ticket, whom one gives it to, and what it means to "get change," even though the arithmetic of getting change may be beyond him. The four- or five-year-old whose mother encourages him to tell the bus driver, even though she is right there, "We want to get off at Second Street," not "I want to get off at Grandma's house," is being helped to take a big step in abstract thinking.

If his family has a telephone, learning to answer it competently and summon the person being called promptly develops poise and the ability to think on one's feet.

Four- and five-year-olds can usually handle such matters with a bit of practice. These, and other challenges that teach them how to deal with the red tape that is involved in the simplest undertakings in our complex society, contribute to children's knowing their way around and tend to make the experience of going to "the big school" less overwhelming.

What Can Parents Teach the Preschooler?

Although mere memorizing that has little or no meaning to the child is not beneficial, encouraging him to think, to be curious, to inquire is highly desirable. Parents have countless opportunities every day to encourage their children to think for themselves. When we turn a question back to a youngster with a friendly "What do *you* think about it?" or "Let's see how much we do know about that" or "Let's find out together," we give him the courage to search for an answer on his own.

Every child does not invariably respond to opportunities we offer him for learning, but we can at least expose him to the opportunities. We can let a youngster set the pace in learning to count, to recognize and name colors, to discover certain fundamental principles about size, weight, shape, roughness or smoothness, wetness or dryness. Differences and correspondences between one object and another also interest him. The four- and five-year-old who has been an eager watcher of some of the children's programs on educational television stations will probably have accumulated a backlog of information of that kind and have become interested in learning to read numbers and letters as well.

The meaning of "more" and "less," "thicker" and "thinner," "heavier" and "lighter," and similar comparisons can be woven into play with the young child or into household tasks he does alongside his mother or father. The discovery that an object has a number of properties is a breakthrough. "This cup is not only red; it is little, it is light, and you can put things in it. Here is a big, green, wooden box that is heavy, but, like the cup, it is made so you can put things in it, too. Now, how about that?" Such discoveries are exciting.

The revelation that two small blocks can fit into the same space as one big one expands the possibilities for using the blocks and also for understanding the relation of the whole to its parts. Adults do this in so many situations every day that we forget how surprising it is to a four- or five-year-old. Jean Piaget, the Swiss psychologist who has contributed so much to our knowledge of how children learn, says that at this age, size, shape, and arrangement of objects confuse a child's comprehension of "how many" and "how much." (Chapter 1 discusses the understanding of the preschooler.) When the child works out for himself the unchangeable fact that whether he has five toy cars in a parking lot he has constructed, or three in the lot and two on the road he has built, he still has five cars, a youngster has had to do some hard thinking.

"How many forks do we need on the table if four of us are eating supper?" The four- or five-year-old is learning more about mathematics if he figures out that four people will need four forks than if he parrots "One and one are two," or even "Ten and ten are twenty" to impress a visiting grandfather.

Kitchens are good science laboratories. For instance, "Here is a nest of cups (or cookie cutters). The little one fits inside the big one. You can't get the big one inside the little one." Obvious? Not to a three-and-a-half-year-old or even to a child a year older.

"Here is a one-quart milk bottle and here is a one-quart mixing bowl, and here is a pitcher with a quart of water in it. If the water in the pitcher fills the bowl, will it fill the bottle?" To most four- and five-year-olds, a tall, narrow receptable seems "bigger" than a low, wide one. It is incomprehensible to them that the same amount of water will fill each. A year or two later that profound truth will be easily grasped. So we do not push for "learning"; we make the experiment a game.

We can also make a game of "I see something blue" (or yellow, or round or square, or three-sided or four-sided), or suggest that children walk around the room and point to as many objects of a certain shape or color as they can find.

Playing with Words

New words can be fun for the small child to try out, and a good vocabulary is an advantage to a first-grader, although the number of words is less important than enjoyment in using them. The discovery that several separate words can describe much the same thing adds range and flexibility to expression. He who can talk about a newly planted tree, for instance, as "small," "tiny," and "low" as well as "little" or "not tall yet" may be experiencing the tree more fully. Whatever points up various ways of saying or doing something tends to widen a child's horizons and make him a bit more at home in the world.

Parents can encourage imaginativeness in using words by asking, "Tell me how this feels" or "How does this look to you?" "What does that sound like?" "How do you feel about it?" These and similar inquiries that stimulate formulation of comparisons or descriptions of objects, sights, sounds, tastes, and smells sharpen budding powers of observation. We may be surprised at how fresh and fluent the children become in their use of language.

Different meanings of the same sounds intrigue the five-year-olds, too. "A pair of shoes" and "a pear that you eat," "a traffic jam" and "strawberry jam" illustrate the variety in language and stretch his mental processes.

We can hardly emphasize often enough in a variety of connections that "There is more than one good way to say things; isn't it more fun that everyone chooses his own way of saying them?" Such emphasis tends to broaden the narrow view a four- or five-year-old has of life and help him make associations more readily.

Classifying Things That Belong Together

Children are bombarded with a welter of information today. Parents can give them some guidelines for sorting out experiences and facts. Just getting the feeling that objects, animals, and sensations can be sorted into appropriate groups is a kind of education that makes learning easier.

We take it for granted, for instance, that beads, cars, or birds can be of various shapes, sizes, or colors and still belong to their respective categories. We lose sight of how puzzling and fascinating this can be to a five-year-old. A robin is one kind of bird and a blue jay is another, but both are birds, because both fly, have feathers, wings, and two legs, and lay eggs. This explanation failed to satisfy one five-year-old, who insisted, "I want to see a bird-bird, not just a robin bird or a black bird. Why isn't there a plain *bird?*" Here is a question that has puzzled philosophers for centuries. What do we mean by the general term, if only particular kinds exist? Young minds need a long time to digest this concept!

The ability to see that what applies to one object or animal or sensation also applies to other slightly different ones in the same general class—in other words, the ability to generalize from a particular instance—is a complicated mental process. A start on using the mind this way will be an invaluable aid to youngsters in school.

Directions Can Be Specific

Since mothers do a great deal of teaching in informal ways, it may be instructive to look at what ways appear to be effective. In another study made by Robert Hess and his associates, the mothers in the experiment were given specific tasks to teach their four-year-olds. First they were to teach the children some simple sorting procedures with blocks. They were then to show the youngsters how to use a toy called "Etch-a-Sketch" to make a simple design. With this toy, lines are made by turning knobs.

After a mother was satisfied that her child could do each task, she left the room, and one of the research staff took over. He asked the child to do the task he had just done with his mother. The conversation between mother and child had been recorded on tape.

The children who performed the tasks well with the research worker were the ones whose mothers had given them specific instructions: "The long block with the X on top goes in the middle" was more effective than vaguer directions, such as, "Fit that one in over there." Also, it was more effective for a mother to praise a correct response than to scold a child for making an incorrect move. In addition, if a mother asked questions or made comments that encouraged the youngster to talk about what he was doing so that she could be sure he understood what was wanted, his learning went along better. "Show me which block has the X on it" or "Can you show me which block is the longest?" impelled the children to function better.

Children's efforts were more successful, too, when their mothers explained the game or the task in words the children could understand. In the "Etch-a-Sketch" knob-turning task, a mother who said "Use the same hand you use to draw with when you turn the knob" was giving her child a direction that had meaning for him. Merely saying "turn the knob" was less effective, especially if she gave no explanation of the fact that turning the knob produced lines and that making lines to "fit together" (or some other phrase that would convey the idea of a design) was "what we want to do."

The desirable teaching methods were not complicated. They would come naturally to many mothers, yet such teaching is sound preparation for following directions in school.

Useful Information for Five-year-olds

Along with the closely intertwined mental, social, and emotional preparation, which has been discussed, a youngster about to enter first grade will need certain practical information.

Most important for any boy or girl venturing beyond his own front door by himself is knowing his full name, not merely that he is called "Brother" or "Fuzzy." His address and telephone number, if the family has a phone, can also be part of his informational baggage.

Many youngsters, when asked their mother's or father's name, answer "Mommy" or "Daddy." They can be taught that other people call them "Mr. and Mrs. James Brown." As an extra precaution, a child may also be taught the name of a relative or close friend of the family who might be called in an emergency if his parents could not be reached. This is especially important if his mother is employed and not readily available during the day.

When a boy or girl uses a pencil or a crayon to draw,

or merely to scribble, we can show him how to hold it properly. That will be a help when he starts to print his name. He may already have learned how to print his name in kindergarten or nursery school, or as a result of watching some educational television program. In any case, being able to do this gives him a good start in first grade. One advantage of being able to read his name is that if we mark his clothes plainly, he can then identify them. That may cut down on losses of caps, mittens, rubbers, sweaters, and such.

Children have usually learned to count at least to ten by the time they enter first grade. Actually, one who is thoroughly at home with the numbers through five has an adequate foundation for being at ease with number work in first grade.

When parents read to a son or daughter, they can point out that the story begins at the top of the page and goes down to the bottom, and that we begin to read at the left and go on to the right. This he will discover for himself if read to often enough, from watching the way our eyes move across the page and noticing the position of the pictures in the book when it is right side up. No harm in explaining it anyway.

Five-year-olds are usually able to dress themselves with no effort, but tying shoe laces may be a bit difficult. In case a boy or girl has not caught on to the knack of tying a bow with a firm knot, we will save him embarrassment if we give him some extra practice in doing so.

A Good Feeling About School

Each child will react to starting school in his own

style. Some are slow to adapt to the new routines and demands but accommodate gradually and steadily. Others appear initially to be taking school in stride but some weeks or months later rebel, invent excuses not to go to school, or show in other ways that they are under real strain.

Some boys and girls do well in the classroom, learn enthusiastically, behave quite cooperatively but at home are irritable, anxious, or more boisterous or quarrelsome than usual. Extra affectionate attention and reassurance to offset the pressures of school are called for when this happens. Since the special virtue of home is that it is a place where one may be "bad" as well as "good," it may, within limits, be more economical emotionally to let off steam at home.

Many first-graders refuse to discuss what goes on at school. They give only the annoying answer, "Nothing," to the daily interrogation, "What happened today at school?" Parents who have seen several children through first grade have discovered it is better not to expect an accounting of what took place each day. "The fewer questions we asked, the more the kids were usually willing to talk," a mother says.

The school and the teachers need parental support. At least the teacher can be given the benefit of the doubt. If we are told she is "mean" or "unfair," we should try to learn what it is the child thinks she does that is "bad." Often it is a misunderstanding or misinterpretation of what she actually said that has caused a young child to become outraged. If we listen to our son's or daughter's retelling of what transpired, we may be able to read between the lines and help our child acquire a better perspective on what actually took place.

Parents need to maintain a delicate balance between upholding their youngster and upholding his teacher. "I won't hear a word against your teacher. She's the boss in school," is as unwise as immediately jumping to our child's defense when he says he has been wronged.

A calm, honest approach to a youngster's complaints is most likely to help him. We can accept the fact that he finds some parts of the school day difficult, some aspects of it threatening—and teachers sometimes unfair. But "It will get better. New things are often hard" is a line that tends to sustain him.

In one family, a timid first-grader began to find school tolerable when her parents proudly displayed on the kitchen wall her paintings and "writing" done at school. Their pride and genuine interest in what she brought home made leaving mother and submitting to the restrictions of the classroom seem worth the effort.

Another mother confesses a mistake she made with her eldest but corrected with the younger ones:

When our eldest started school, I often said to her, "Now that you are big enough to go to school, you are big enough to go upstairs to bed at night alone," or "Now that you are in school, you are big enough to help me more," and so on. I kept expecting all sorts of new steps forward, when what she needed was a chance to slide back and have a bit more support from us at home. She was putting all she had into getting along at school and didn't have the energy, physically or emotionally, to meet more demands at home.

Taking it for granted that every child goes to school —on time, every day (mostly)—that what one learns there is important, and being matter-of-fact but firm about this helps a boy or girl accommodate in time to what is expected of him in his new life. Most of all, reassurance that this first-grader will be able to be "a good learner," will like school, and that his parents are pleased with him and standing by him, supports him through this major transition.

Bibliography and Suggested Reading

1 The Delightful Age

Almy, Milly. *Young Children's Thinking: Studies of Some Aspects of Piaget's Theory*. New York: Teachers College Press, 1966.

Baldwin, Alfred. *Theories of Child Development*. New York: John Wiley & Sons, Inc., 1967.

Erikson, Erik H. *Childhood and Society*. New York: W. W. Norton & Co., Inc., 1950.

French, Edward L., M.D., and Scott, J. Clifford, M.D. *How You Can Help Your Retarded Child: A Manual for Parents*. Philadelphia: J. B. Lippincott & Co., 1967.
The development, nature, and needs of the mentally retarded child are presented by experienced and compassionate medical men, one of them a psychiatrist, who have directed the famous Devereux School.

Gesell, Arnold, M.D., and Ilg, Frances, M.D. *Infant and Child in the Culture of Today*. New York: Harper, 1943.
"The culture of today" is far different from that of 1943, and some of the features of a child's day as described in this classic volume are so outmoded as to be almost quaint. Yet physical development and patterns of growth have not changed, and the description of these is still valid.

Hoffman, Martin L., and Wladis, Lois. *Child Development Research*. vol. I. New York: Russell Sage Foundation, 1964.

Inhelder, B., and Piaget, J. *The Growth of Logical Thinking from Childhood to Adolescence.* New York: Basic Books, Inc., 1957.

Kagan, J., and Moss, H. A. *Birth to Maturity.* New York: John Wiley & Sons, Inc., 1962.

Landreth, Catherine. *Early Childhood.* Alfred A. Knopf, Inc., 1967.

Linton, Ralph. "Status and Role." In *The Study of Man.* New York: Appleton & Co., 1936.

Murphy, Lois B. *The Widening World of Childhood.* New York: Basic Books, Inc., 1962.

Pearce, Jane, M.D., and Newton, Saul. *The Conditions of Human Growth.* New York: Citadel Press, Inc., 1969.

Spock, Benjamin, M.D., and Lerrigo, Marion O. *Caring for Your Disabled Child.* New York: The Macmillan Co., Inc., 1965.

Stone, L. Joseph, and Church, Joseph. *Childhood and Adolescence.* 2d ed. New York: Random House, 1968.

Stuart, Harold C., and Prugh, Daniel G., ed. *The Healthy Child.* Boston: Harvard University Press, 1960.

Toffler, Alvin. *Future Shock.* New York: Bantam Books, Inc., 1970.

Winnicott, D. W. *The Child, the Family and the Outside World.* New York: Penguin Books, Inc., 1970.

2 When There Are Siblings—and When There Are None

Gehman, Betsy Holland. *Twins: Twice the Trouble, Twice the Fun.* Philadelphia: J. B. Lippincott Co., 1965.

Gilmore, J. B. "Birth Order and Social Reinforcers of Effectiveness in Children." *Child Development* 35:193–200.

LeShan, Eda J. *The Only Child.* New York: Public Affairs Pamphlets, 1960.

Neisser, Edith G. *Brothers and Sisters.* New York: Harper, 1951.

308

———. *The Eldest Child.* New York: Harper, 1957.

Scheinfeld, Amram. *Twins and Supertwins.* Philadelphia: J. B. Lippincott Co., 1967.

The relationship of twins to each other and to the other children in the family is discussed in helpful, reassuring terms.

Simon, Anne W. *Stepchildren in the Family: A View of Children in Remarriage.* New York: Pocket Books, 1964.

3 Helping Your Child Get Along with Others

Bronfenbrenner, Urie. *Two Worlds of Childhood: U.S. and U.S.S.R.* New York: Russell Sage Foundation, 1970.

Freud, Anna. *Research at the Hampstead Child Therapy Clinic and Other Papers.* London: Hogarth, 1970.

Hoover, Mary, and Mayer, Greta. *Learning to Love and Let Go.* New York: Child Study Association, 1965.

La Crosse, Robert E. *Day Care for America's Children.* New York: Public Affairs Pamphlets, 1971.

Members of the Staff of The Boston Children's Medical Center, and Gregg, Elizabeth M. *What to Do When "There's Nothing to Do."* New York: Delacorte Press, 1967.

Piers, Maria W. *Growing Up with Children.* Chicago: Quadrangle, 1966.

The section on "Animals in the Life of the Child" describes the part live pets can play in the development of sociability and ability to relate oneself to others.

4 Contrariness, and All That

Hartley, Ruth E., and Goldenson, Robert M. *The Complete Book of Children's Play.* Rev. ed. New York: Thomas Y. Crowell, 1963.

Hoover, Mary, and Mayer, Greta. *When Children Need Special Help with Emotional Problems.* New York: Child Study Association, 1961.

The sections on "Danger Signals" and "When Does a Signal Need Further Attention" are particularly helpful if one is in doubt about a child's development.

Roy, K. "Parents' Attitude Toward Their Children." *Journal of Home Economics*, 1950, 42:652–653.

Sears, R. R.; Maccoby, E. E.; and Levin, H. *Patterns of Child Rearing*. New York: Harper, 1957.

Siegelman, Marvin. "College Students' Personality Correlates of Early Parent-Child Relationships." *Journal of Consulting Psychology*, 1965, 29:558–564.

Spock, Benjamin, M.D. *Problems of Parents*. Boston: Houghton Mifflin Co., 1962.

5 Questions Need Honest Answers

Bruner, Jerome. *On Knowing: Essays for the Left Hand*. New York: Athenaeum, 1969.

Despert, J. Louise, M.D. *Children of Divorce*. New York: Doubleday & Co., Inc., 1953.

You will find help in answering children's questions about divorce in their own family or among the parents of their friends, as well as assistance in meeting this crisis.

Wolf, Anna M. W. *Helping Your Child to Understand Death*. New York: The Child Study Association of America, Inc., 1958.

This sensitive guide, written in question-and-answer form, goes to the heart of the problem of answering children's questions about death.

6 Masculinity . . . Femininity

Benedek, Therese, M.D., and Anthony, James E., M.D. *Parenthood: Its Psychology and Psychopathology*. New York: Little Brown & Co., 1970.

Bennett, G. K., and Cohen, L. R. "Men and Women: Personality Patterns and Contrasts." *Genetic Psychology Monographs*, 1959, 60:101–153.

Fraiberg, Selma. *The Magic Years*. New York: Charles Scribner's Sons, 1959.

Graubart, Stephen, ed. "The Woman in America." *Daedalus*, 1964, 93:2.

Howe, Florence. "Sexual Stereotypes Start Early." *Saturday Review*, October 16, 1971, 76 ff.

Lewis, Harvey Alvin. "The Effect of Shedding the First Deciduous Tooth upon the Passing of the Oedipus Complex." *American Psychoanalytic Journal*, 1958, 6:5–37.

Marmor, Judd, M.D. *Sexual Inversion: The Multiple Roots of Homosexuality*. New York: Basic Books, Inc., 1965.
This book, somewhat scientific in tone and not too easy to read, emphasizes that homosexuality cannot be attributed to any one factor in a child's life.

Rossi, Alice. "Women in Science—Why So Few?" *Science*, 1965, CXLVIII: 1197–1202.

Rothbart, Mary K., and Maccoby, Eleanor. "Parents' Differential Reactions to Sons and Daughters." *Journal of Personality and Social Psychology*, 1966, 4:237–243.

Vidal, Gore. "In Another Country." *New York Review of Books*, 1971, XVII, 1:8–12.

Wyden, Peter and Barbara. *Growing Up Straight: What Every Thoughtful Parent Should Know About Homosexuality*. New York: Stein & Day, Inc., 1968.
This book emphasizes how many different forces go into shaping heterosexuality and homosexuality.

7 Toward a Healthy Conscience

Fraiberg, Selma. *The Magic Years*. New York: Charles Scribner's Sons, 1959.
Although the book does not take up material that is not touched on in this or other chapters, the section on "The Dawn of Conscience" is so outstanding that every parent should be familiar with it. The pages dealing with "Acquisition of Moral Values" are particularly helpful.

8 Fears

Berger, Allan S., M.D. "Anxiety in Young Children." *Young Children*, 1970, XXVII, 1:5–17.

Hirsch, Selma. *The Fears Men Live By*. New York: Harper, 1955.
This book discusses some of the groundless fears that shape our thinking and where they come from.

Overstreet, Bonaro. *Understanding Fear in Ourselves and Others*. New York: Harper, 1951.
The first five chapters of Part I are valuable in understanding and helping a child cope with his fear.

Ross, Helen. *Fears of Children*. New York: Science Research Associates, 1951.

―――. *The Shy Child*. New York: Public Affairs Pamphlets, 1953.

9 Encouraging Independence

Boston Children's Hospital Medical Center staff. *Accident Handbook: A New Approach to Children's Safety*. Pamphlet. New York: Dell Publishing Co., Inc., 1966.

Hess, Robert D., and Shipman, Virginia. *Cognitive Elements in Maternal Behavior*. Unpublished report of research. Chicago: University of Chicago, 1967.

Moore, James E. "Antecedents of Dependency and Autonomy in Young Children." *Dissertation Abstracts*, 1965, 26:1966.

10 Minor Annoyances and Larger Worries

Arnstein, Helene, in cooperation with the Child Study Association of America, Inc. *What to Tell Your Child About Birth, Death, Illness, Divorce, and Other Family Crises*. New York: Pocket Books, 1964.
This extremely helpful book has sections on many of the "larger worries," such as the illness of a parent and the divorce or remarriage of parents.

Brazelton, T. Berry, M.D. Interview. *Chicago Today*, Oct. 19, 1971.

Geist, Harold. A *Child Goes to the Hospital*. Springfield: Chas. Thomas, 1965.
Helpful suggestions to parents for preparing a child for going to the hospital and accommodating himself to hospital routines.

Goldman, R., and Shanes, G. H. "Comparisons of the Goals That Parents of Stutterers and Parents of Non-stutterers Set for Their Children." *Journal of Speech and Hearing Disorders*, 1964, 29:381–389.

Kinster, Donald B. "Covert and Overt Maternal Rejection in Stuttering." *Journal of Speech and Hearing Disorders*, 1961, 26:145–155.

McCord, W.; McCord, J.; and Zola, I. K. *Origins of Crime*. New York: Columbia University Press, 1959.

Randall, Margaret. *The Home Encyclopedia of Moving Your Family*. New York: Berkley Publishing Corp., 1959.

Siegel, A. E. "Film-mediated Fantasy-aggression: Strength of Aggressive Drive." *Child Development*, 1956, 27: 365–378.

11 Preparing Your Child for School

Association for Childhood Education. *Feelings and Learning*. New York: International, 1965.
A collection of essays by some of the foremost authorities on early childhood education, among them Lois Barclay Murphy, Dorothy E. M. Gardner, Anna Freud, Merle E. Bonney, and Laura Hopper.

Beyer, Evelyn. *Teaching Young Children*. New York: Pegasus, 1968.
If you have been confused about the methods as well as the strengths and weaknesses of various theories of nursery school education, this book offers clarification. It can be as useful to parents as to nursery school teachers.

Eckstein, Rudolph. "Parents and Teachers: Who Does What?" Address delivered at a seminar, Nov. 3, 1966, of the North Shore Mental Health Association, Winnetka, Ill.

Harvey, O. J.; Hunt, D. E.; and Shroder, H. M. *Conceptual Systems and Personality Organization.* New York: John Wiley & Sons, Inc., 1961.

Hymes, James L., Jr. *Teaching the Child Under Six.* Columbus, Ohio: Merrill, 1968.

Not all the material in this book applies directly to preparing a child for school, but this respected educator's ideas about teaching a child to read before he enters first grade are interesting and convincing.

Mote, Florence B. "The Relationship Between Child Self-concept in School and Parental Attitudes and Behavior in Child Rearing." *Dissertation Abstracts,* 1967, 27:3319.

Pickard, P. M. *The Activity of Children.* New York: Humanities Press, Inc., 1965.

Not entirely easy reading, but worth the effort, because the author makes it clear that children learn best through discovery.

Additional Reading

Albrecht, Margaret. *Parents and Teen-agers: Getting Through to Each Other.* New York: Parents' Magazine Press, 1972.

Gilbert, Sara D. *Three Years to Grow.* New York: Parents' Magazine Press, 1972.

Hoover, Mary B. *The Responsive Parent.* New York: Parents' Magazine Press, 1972.

Minton, Lynn. *Growing into Adolescence.* New York: Parents' Magazine Press, 1972.

Mogal, Doris P. *Character in the Making.* New York: Parents' Magazine Press, 1972.

Index